Language & Literacy

Carol Rushing Carr

Pre-K Teacher's Guide

····SCHOOL

····IS

COOL!

8001 MacArthur Blvd
Cabin John, MD 20818
301.263.2700
getsetforschool.com

Authors: Jan Z. Olsen, OTR and Emily F. Knapton, M. Ed., OTR/L
Illustrators: Jan Z. Olsen, OTR and Julie Koborg
Curriculum Designers: Carolyn Satoh, Kate McGill, Cheryl Lundy Warfield, Suzanne Belahmira, Allessandra Bradley-Burns, Mónica Palacio, Adina Rosenthal, Robert Walnock
Graphic Designers: Jodi Dudek, Nichole Monaghan

Copyright © 2011 Get Set for School®
First Edition
ISBN: 978-1-934825-30-3
123456789Webcrafters161514
Printed in the U.S.A.

The Get Set for School® program and teacher's guides are intuitive and packed with resources and information. Nevertheless, we are constantly developing new ideas and content that make the program easier to teach and to learn.

To make this information available to you, we created a password-protected section of our website exclusively for users of this teacher's guide. Here you'll find new tips, in-depth information about topics described in this guide, other instructional resources, and material you can share with students, parents, and other educators.

Just go to **getsetforschool.com/click** and enter your passcode: **TGLL11**

Enjoy the online resources, and send us any input that you think would be helpful to others: janolsen@getsetforschool.com

Dear Educator,

Welcome to the Get Set for School® Language & Literacy program, which is just right for Pre-K children. You may know us from our Readiness & Writing program. If you do, your children are building letters with Wood Pieces, learning how to hold crayons, writing capitals and numbers, and singing "The Ant, the Bug and the Bee." Of course they know and love Mat Man®.

Whether you are a long time fan or brand new to Get Set for School, we know you'll enjoy this Pre-K Language & Literacy program. It's child-friendly and developmentally based. This program will also fit into your day and your way of teaching. You'll find that the materials and activities in this program will help you stimulate and sustain learning.

This Language & Literacy program will suit your children and grow with them. You probably know that Get Set for School was started by occupational therapists who know and understand the readiness skills needed for later school success. We have high expectations, but we make learning accessible from the very first day. Now we have literacy and early childhood experts working with us. Together we've designed products, hands-on activities, and teaching strategies to boost language and literacy skills in the same active, child-friendly way.

This program respects children's need for self-directed play, while still responsibly preparing them for kindergarten. This guide is organized by Pre-K teaching domains and learning skills/benchmarks so you can have confidence your children are well prepared to meet kindergarten expectations. At the same time, we treasure children's natural curiosity and creativity. We respect what children already know and how much they learn independently. You'll find many suggestions for keeping their learning active and joyful.

We hope you have a wonderful year—a year in which learning and teaching is truly a joy.

All the best,

Emily F. Knapton   *Jan Z. Olsen*

Emily F. Knapton and Jan Z. Olsen

Table of Contents

Getting to Know Get Set for School®

Using Your Language & Literacy Pre-K Teacher's Guide

Pre-K Classroom & Children

1 - Phonological Awareness
I Hear It and Say It!

2 - Alphabet Knowledge
Letters, Letters, Letters

Getting to Know Get Set for School®

Get Set for School Pre-K Philosophies and Principles

We know how children learn best and how to prepare them for school. We took our years of experience and the most relevant research about how children learn best to develop this award-winning curriculum for school readiness.

Different and Better

We understand that preschoolers learn through movement and participation. They need explicit modeled instruction. They also need playful learning opportunities to explore and internalize new ideas. Our playful approach is at the heart of our success. Young children are not ready to sit still and focus for long periods of time. They learn best when they move, manipulate objects, build, sing, draw, and participate in dramatic play. Preschoolers need instruction tailored to their different styles of learning. You need tools to meet these needs. Our unique Pre-K programs make teaching easy and rewarding for you with:

- Research based approach that addresses different learning styles
- Developmental progression that builds on what children already know
- Friendly voice that connects with children
- Multisensory lessons that break difficult concepts into simple tasks
- Hands-on materials that make children want to learn

What and How We Teach

Eager - Children learn naturally through everyday experiences with people, places, and things. They are excited to learn and actively explore and experiment. They are born imitators and scientists who thrive on active hands-on interaction with the physical world. They learn through play and through physical and sensory experiences. The materials throughout the learning space affect how children feel, what they do, and how they learn. Our products (music and manipulatives) invite eager children to learn.

Able - The child is learning the core competencies of the culture—how we read, write, and do math. We actively and deliberately fill the day with what we want children to learn. We build familiarity and competency with the music that we play, the words that we use, and the way in which we use materials and teach lessons. Our materials and lessons are flexible so that you can teach in a developmental sequence from simpler to more complex. This approach ensures that children develop as confident, independent problem solvers and learners.

Social - Pre-K is social and challenging. The child is learning how to work and play with others. We use music and hands-on materials to encourage inclusive participation and the development of social, physical, language, math, and early readiness skills. We read, draw, sing, build, and dance with children, enticing them to join us on a learning adventure. Our materials also encourage family involvement to continue learning at home. Many activities have take-home components to encourage children to form connections between learning in school and home situations.

A Developmental Curriculum

Preschoolers will enter your classroom with different and continually evolving abilities. They will not all be ready developmentally to learn the same skills at the same time.

To meet the needs of Pre-K children, a curriculum must be accessible at all points within this wide spectrum of needs and skills. It should invite participation, build a base of understanding, and challenge children's thinking. You need support to meet all your students where they are as they develop throughout the year.

We teach in developmental order by starting at the level that does not assume prior knowledge or competency. We enable children to excel by respecting their present level of development and building from there.

Children need to learn certain skills explicitly. We teach them how to read, write, and count. We help them to recognize, name, and write letters and numbers. We teach them how to listen for and say sounds. We also teach them important social skills.

Supporting Parents and Teachers

Parents are a child's first and most important teachers. Our materials encourage family involvement to continue learning activities at home. Lessons sometimes ask families to lend items from home to personalize activities. Many of the activities have take-home components to encourage children to form connections between home and school.

Some of our materials are also designed to be taken home and shared with families as children practice skills learned in school, show their families what they are learning, and ask for their help and participation.

Get Set for School makes a seamless transition between home and school. We recognize that preschool often is a child's first experience away from home. Our activities encourage children to share family experiences and see how those become part of learning in school. Our curriculum also acknowledges and celebrates cultural differences.

Get Set for School® – Three Core Learning Areas

Get Set for School is a curriculum that prepares young learners for school with three complete programs: Readiness & Writing, Language & Literacy, and Numbers & Math. These programs complement and expand your existing Pre-K program. You engage children with the following strategies:

- Creative lessons that enable children of different abilities to achieve
- Child-friendly language and activities
- Developmentally based teaching that works at every level
- Hands-on approach that promotes active participation

Readiness & Writing

This program is the core of Get Set for School. The handwriting component is based on more than 25 years of success with Handwriting Without Tears®. Writing requires many skills that are essential for school: physical, language, cognitive, social, and perceptual. Our Readiness & Writing program uses music, movement, and multisensory manipulatives to teach all the core readiness skills, including crayon grip, letter and number recognition, number and capital letter formation, and body awareness.

Language & Literacy

This program is a wonderful complement to our Get Set for School Readiness & Writing program. We use dramatic play, singing, finger plays, manipulatives, and movement to teach children to rhyme, clap syllables, make and break compound words, and identify sounds. We expose children to rich literature (see Book Connection on page 180) to foster a love of reading, build vocabulary, and learn how books work. They learn facts from informational text. They learn to use new words and develop oral language skills by listening, retelling, and narrating stories. They also learn that there is meaning in the words they say as they watch teachers write what they say.

Numbers & Math

This program is a natural extension of our Get Set for School readiness program and helps children build number sense right from the start. We use manipulatives, music, and rhymes, to teach counting, comparisons, spatial awareness, patterning, sequencing, matching, sorting, problem solving, and even Pre-K geometry skills. Lessons give children time to play with real objects and test their ideas so that math becomes real and meaningful. Children also develop oral language that helps them learn about and express math concepts.

Using Your Teacher's Guide

Curriculum Organization: Domains and Learning Skills/Benchmarks

Are you concerned about meeting Pre-K standards while still keeping Pre-K playful and fun? We have a solution for you. We sought out top literacy experts, studied the "literacy lingo," and incorporated all of the Pre-K literacy standards. The result: an educator-friendly literacy guide. We created our *Language & Literacy Pre-K Teacher's Guide* with the Pre-K teacher and parent in mind. We turned the educational jargon into simple explanations and fun activities while covering all of the essential skills. We think that you and your children will enjoy the many literacy activities that we have created.

Research tells us that preschoolers should develop understanding in six literacy domains, or skill areas. These learning skills are also called benchmarks. This guide includes two versions of benchmarks. One set is what we refer to as friendly titles. These are found in the table of contents, on the first page of each domain, and in the skill descriptions on the left side of each activity page. The second version is written in more formal academic language. These are the benchmarks you will see in the Look What We're Learning sections. The complete list can be found in the Resources section of this teacher's guide.

The learning skills within each domain are organized in developmental order, from the easiest to the more challenging. Our lessons have a main activity and two activity variations for each small skill. There are also activities to support English language learners and children who need more help with each lesson.

Through play and explicit instruction, children develop early literacy skills in these six domains:

1. Phonological Awareness
2. Alphabet Knowledge
3. Concepts About Print
4. Comprehension
5. Oral Language
6. Writing

You may not be an expert in these literacy domains, but as you read this teacher's guide and work with our activities, you will become more confident. Here are some plain talk explanations of each domain.

Phonological Awareness

Phonological awareness is the ability to hear and manipulate parts of spoken language. As children develop, they begin to make sense of the different sounds and words they hear. Research shows that phonological awareness is a critical early literacy skill and impacts later reading success. All children can benefit from phonological awareness instruction whether they are learning a skill for the first time or practicing a skill they may already understand.

Alphabet Knowledge

Alphabet knowledge is the ability to name the letters of the alphabet and recognize letters in print. Alphabet recognition is one of the most accurate predictors of early reading success (Johnston, 2004). Our activities address the broad range of alphabet experiences and knowledge in your classroom.

Concepts About Print

To learn to read, children must learn how books work and develop what educators call Concepts About Print. These concepts include: 1) the parts of a book - front, back, spine, title, author and illustrator; 2) how to hold a book right-side up; 3) how to turn pages from front to back; and 4) how to read from top to bottom and left to right. Children's knowledge of these concepts when they enter kindergarten is a major factor in determining their literacy level (Nichols, Rupley, Rickleman, & Algozzine, 2004).

Comprehension

Comprehension is grasping the meaning of what is spoken or read. But what does it mean for Pre-K children? Infants begin to make sense of things, or make meaning, within days of being born. Pre-K children try to make meaning from what they hear, see, and experience. They make meaning from stories that are read to them, through self-directed play, and through dramatic play.

Oral Language

Oral language is children's ability to listen and express themselves. Children begin to learn language from birth. As they grow and develop, so do their language skills. Pre-K children learn to understand and use language to express their feelings, thoughts, and observations. These skills are key to the development of reading and writing skills (Burns, Griffin, & Snow, 1999; Strickland & Morrow, 1988; Weaver, 1988). They learn new vocabulary words and develop oral language skills by social interaction and listening to, retelling, and narrating stories.

Writing

When you think about writing in Pre-K, you probably don't think of story creation and sentence writing. But young children enjoy creating stories and seeing their words become print. You, as the teacher, are the scribe, and the children are the authors. Pre-K is a time for seeing how spoken words are written. It's also a time for both play writing and beginning writing instruction.

Getting Acquainted

You may be new to Get Set for School® and using just our Language & Literacy program. Or you may be a long-time Get Set for School user with all of our materials. Either way, you'll find our products and teaching tips to be fun and effective.

This teacher's guide is intuitive, easy to work with, and full of "aha" moments. Here's a quick orientation:

Domain Introductions – Each domain begins with a simple explanation of that learning area and lists the domain's specific skills in developmental order.

Multisensory Language and Literacy Products – Our hands-on products are at the heart of our success. Each product is introduced on its own page and in the domain where it is used most. We may use a product in other domains (sometimes before it has been introduced). If you want to learn more about a specific product, here is a quick guide to where you can find those introductions:

Sing, Sound & Count With Me CD – pages 26–27

Sound Around Box™ – page 28

Line It Up™ (Letter Cards) – page 62, (Story Cards) – page 104, (Coloring Cards) – page 152

A-B-C Touch & Flip® Cards – page 64

My Book – page 88

Word Time™ – page 132

Discovery Teaching in Your Day – Next to every product page is a Discovery Teaching page. It's a quick introduction to a variety of teaching strategies: Old Favorites, the tried and true teaching strategies used for years with great success; Have You Tried These, some strategies that you may not know, but that we particularly like; and Mix In Some Get Set For School Activities, other playful ways to use these products in your teaching.

Other Get Set For School Products – You'll notice that we occasionally refer to products from our Numbers & Math or Readiness & Writing program. They work so well in some situations that we just had to bring them in. If you don't have them, you may want to consider them, or use tools you already have in your classroom.

Activities – See pages 12–13 for a layout of our activity pages—the bulk of this teacher's guide. You will find the activities intuitive, child friendly, and effective for teaching important skills.

Resources – At the end of the book, you'll find useful resources that you will want to review during those quieter moments when children are out of the classroom.

Teaching Guidelines – We are sticklers for developmentally based instruction (going from easy to more challenging), but there are many ways to use our products and stay true to developmental principles. Our products can work on multiple levels. We offer Teaching Guidelines to help organize your thinking/lessons.

Choosing Activities in this Teacher's Guide

The activities in this teacher's guide are organized by domain in developmentally progressive order. Here are four ways to choose activities within a domain:

1. **Choose what your children like.** Happy, engaged children are learning. It's fine to repeat favorite activities. Be sure to try the additional activities in the More to Learn section to vary or extend activities.

2. **Choose what your children need.** If you know children haven't been read to, or had experience with counting, blocks, shape sorters, and puzzles, give them that exposure and those experiences at school. Be sure to use the ELL and Support sections to meet the needs of English language learners and children who need any extra help or support. The activities in the ELL and Support sections are motivating and hands-on so you can use them with children of different abilities and backgrounds.

3. **Choose what fits into your theme.** If you are using a theme approach, turn to the index on pages 202–203 to select the activities that will support the theme.

4. **Choose a range of activities.** Refer to the Pre-K Teaching Guidelines on pages 186–195. These guidelines help you organize activities. However, you may re-order the activities to suit your children/teaching.

Even with the most thoughtful choice, some activities may surprise you when you try them. Here's what you may learn:

- **They're not ready.** There is no harm in trying. If an activity doesn't suit your children, put it away for another day.
- **They're almost ready.** This could work with simple tweaking or with a few more tries. Perhaps you'll choose a simpler, related activity. Have them try a concept naturally through self-directed play. You may be pleasantly surprised as children discover things on their own.
- **They are ready.** This activity suits them perfectly and can be repeated. Be sure to use the exercises in the "More to Learn" section to vary and extend the activity.

Activity Design

Skill Timeline – This shows where each skill fits into the progression of skills. Large dot indicates skill being taught.

Title of Lesson – See next page for detailed description.

Skill – This is the skill being taught in this activity.

Description of the Skill – Important information about the skill is outlined for you.

Pictures – Illustrations or graphics give you a visual representation of the learning activity.

Look What We're Learning – The language and literacy benchmarks addressed by the main activity are listed. We've also included social-emotional and sensory motor benchmarks.

Make Predictions   Recognize Beginning, Middle, and End

What Will Happen?

Make Predictions
When children can predict, they can better link prior knowledge, observation, thinking, and active listening. Children use illustrations and prior knowledge to make predictions. They ask questions, make guesses, and draw conclusions. This approach to reading engages children in the story and boosts comprehension.

Look What We're Learning

Comprehension
- Make a prediction about a book by looking at pictures and illustrations
- Use prior knowledge to make predictions about a story
- Listen to learn what happened in a story
- Listen to converse with an adult or peer

Vocabulary

predict
prediction
title

106 *Comprehension*   © 2011 Get Set for School®

Domain – The domain is listed at the bottom of the page to help you quickly identify what you are teaching.

Vocabulary – When new vocabulary is introduced, you will find this section. Definitions can be found in the glossary.

What Will Happen?

Title of Lesson – Each lesson has a creative title describing the activity. You can also find the title of the lesson at the bottom of the page and before the skill description.

Materials/Setup:
• Children's book

Grouping:
Small group; Whole class

English Language Learners:
Before you do the activity, preview the objects in the book's illustrations. Have children repeat the names of the objects. When you do the activity, children will be more familiar with the vocabulary and story.

Objective
Children predict what will happen in a story.

Objective – This is the goal of the main activity.

Activity
I am going to read a book. Before I read, let's predict what will happen. Predict means to tell what will happen before we really know.

1. Show children the front cover. **What do you see in the picture? What do you predict will happen in this story?** Listen, and ask why children made their predictions. Write down the predictions if you like.

2. Read the title. **Now that you know the title, what do you predict will happen? Did your prediction change?**

3. Begin reading aloud. Stop once or twice to get any new or updated predictions.

4. Review the children's predictions after reading. Compare them with what really happened. **What did we predict, or say would happen? What really happened?**

Activity – The main activity tells you what to do in simple steps.

✓ Check for Understanding
Notice how and why the children make their predictions. Do their predictions make sense? Do their predictions change based on additional information?

Check for Understanding – This is an informal measure of a child's understanding of the main activity.

Support: Show Line It Up™ Story Card 1 from "Isabel's Birthday." Have children predict what will happen. Read the story.

Support – This section provides guidance on how to meet the needs of children who may have difficulty grasping the skill.

More to Learn

Pumpkin Life
Use "Growing Pumpkins" Story Cards from Line It Up. Show each picture and ask for predictions. Have children predict what is growing. Read the title and story after predictions have been made.

It's in the Name
For a challenge, have children predict what will happen after only hearing the title of the story. Have them draw pictures showing their predictions and talk about them. Then read the story. For more fun, have children dictate a new story with that title.

More to Learn – This section provides additional activities to vary and extend the main activity.

Materials/Setup – Suggested items you will need to gather for the main activity are listed. Materials for Support, English Language Learners, and More to Learn are listed within those sections.

Grouping – The recommended number of children for the main activity is indicated.

English Language Learners – Each lesson has a strategy to support English language learners.

Hands-On Products

We are excited to introduce our new literacy products. This is just a preview of each product. You can find an in-depth overview of each product within the various domains of this teacher's guide.

My Book

My Book is a child's personal storybook and a special way to explore the wonders of books and words. Children draw themselves into pictures and share their own experiences about people, places, and things. Children learn about the parts of the book inside and out, develop oral language, and build vocabulary. What better way to learn about books than writing and reading about yourself? See page 88.

Word Time™

Word Time uses the magic of words to build strong vocabulary and oral language skills. Preschoolers develop new vocabulary around meaningful subjects and engage in word-related, hands-on activities. See page 132.

Sound Around Box™

Sound Around Box holds many surprises and gives you easy ways to teach letters, rhyming, syllables, listening, cooperation, and much more. See page 28.

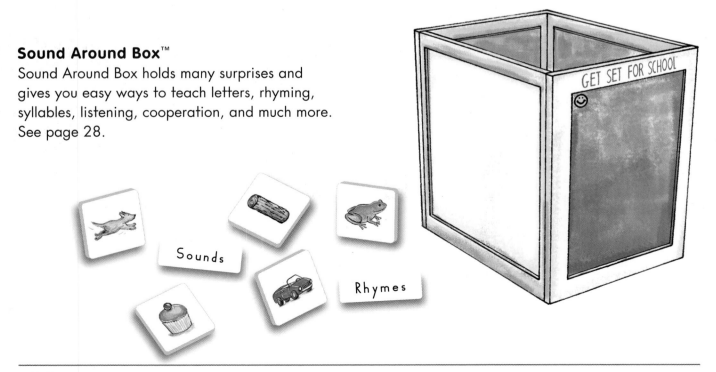

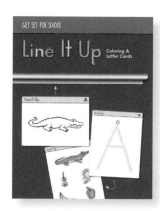

Line It Up™

Line It Up invites children to tell stories, color pictures, and explore letters. The Story Cards use three pictures to teach beginning, middle, and end of five different stories. The Letter and Coloring Card activities encourage children to discuss their ideas, build vocabulary, and practice important comprehension and phonological awareness skills. See pages 62, 104, and 152.

A-B-C Touch & Flip® Cards

A-B-C Touch & Flip Cards provide a multisensory learning experience. Double sided cards feature tactile letters and a puzzle to teach letter recognition, alphabet sequencing, and capital/lowercase matching. The flip feature helps children check their work. See page 64.

Mat Man Book Set

The Mat Man book series is a delightful way to teach language and readiness skills. It also introduces children to a broader world of discovery.

Sing, Sound & Count With Me CD

Sing, Sound & Count With Me CD is filled with fun songs about math, literacy, and life both inside and outside the Pre-K classroom. See page 26.

Pre-K Classroom & Children

Classroom Environment

Your classroom environment reflects many things about you and your teaching. An environment where children know where to locate items, what comes next in the day, and why they are participating in various activities provides structure and builds security. A cheerful, well-organized classroom helps you to teach effectively and allows your students easy access to the toys and materials that will help them grow and learn.

Social Environment

Provide a welcome environment where all of the children feel accepted and part of the classroom community. Teaching and modeling ways to share, resolve conflict, and speak kindly to one another helps children learn and play with others. This, in turn, builds self-confidence.

Physical Setup

A good classroom setup promotes desired learning and behavior. Make sure the setup of your room offers a range of play and learning places. Set up the space and place materials intentionally to promote discovery play and learning. During teacher-directed times, make sure your students are situated so they can easily see and hear you. It's also important that children can participate easily in the activities during group exercises. Enhance learning in Pre-K with an organized space for teaching, working, and playing. Some ideas include:

- Dramatic play centers: kitchen, garage, store, and so forth with related play materials
- Large spaces for independent, self-directed play and learning
- Spacious active play area that allows free movement and participation in large group activities such as dance and whole group exercises
- Appropriately sized tables and chairs that allow you to position your students well for table activities
- Sensory and art centers such as easels, sand and/or water tables

Materials

There is a wide range of developmentally appropriate materials for Pre-K teachers to choose from. Every now and then, replace the materials in your room to offer new experiences. As you add things to your classroom, discuss the additions with your students. They can participate in how materials are set up and stored. Child friendly labels with pictures/colors/words will help them locate, sort, organize, and return objects to their proper places in the room. A good digital camera can come in handy during field trips or when you are designing classroom activities.

Walls

Walls can work for you because they can define spaces and support learning. They can also work against you if you display every good picture because you'll have chaos and disorder. Use your walls actively and selectively.

Walls are for the children. Choose signs and labels to help them understand the purpose of print and to recognize letters and numbers. Instead of posting teaching standards or adult information on precious wall space, find an alternate area where that information is easily accessible to adults.

Fine art posters, paintings, and arrangements add visual beauty to your room and increase cultural appreciation and awareness. You can vary permanent and changing displays to create interest. Display these at children's eye level to spark curiosity and wonder. Art shows emotion and introduces unfamiliar places and things. Talk about the art displayed around the classroom to add to children's background knowledge.

Audio

Every Pre-K classroom needs music. Music encourages movement and movement helps promote learning. Children benefit from music as they explore and play. Be considerate of children who are sensitive to noise. Use a low volume when you are asking children to focus on other work. Consider the wealth of our musical heritage. Include classical, jazz, country, and other genres—as well as children's music. Music is an important part of culture because the language, rhythms, and instruments introduce children to other times and places. Rhythmic and melodic patterns in music reinforce math understanding through multiple sensory channels.

Developmental Stages for Language & Literacy: Two- & Three-Year Olds

Outside   Did you know that bringing children along on errands promotes literacy? Point to everyday items like signs, colors, and letters to build background knowledge and boost vocabulary. Talk about things that interest children to develop their language skills.

Inside   Spend time with books to promote love of learning and reading. Books allow children to experience the world in a different way. Books build vocabulary, teach rhythm and rhyme, and foster early comprehension skills.

2-year-old

10–40 words; 2-word phrases

Books, Rhymes, Finger Plays, Songs
- Enjoys books, points to pictures
- Begins to join in familiar songs/rhymes
- Makes some animals sounds—moo, baa

Talking
- Doesn't always make sense to strangers
- Asks for food by name: milk, juice
- Answers familiar questions with gestures or words

Thinking and behavior
- Gives an object—"Hand me the spoon."
- Follows a simple direction—"Shut the door."
- Unclear about fantasy/reality

Word Use
- Tells actions with verbs—run, hop
- Uses personal pronouns—me, mine

3-year-old

40–200 words; 3-word phrases

Books, Rhymes, Finger Plays, Songs
- Holds books right-side up, turns pages one by one
- Pretend reads a familiar book
- Knows familiar songs/nursery rhymes

Talking
- Doesn't always make sense to strangers
- Asks many "Why?" questions
- Answers simple "Where?" "What?" questions

Thinking and Behavior
- Puts or finds object as directed
- Begins to share, passes things to another
- Plays pretend with others
- Sorts by attributes—blocks, balls

Word Use
- Adds "s" to make any plural
- Adds "ed" to any verb for past tense
- Describes with words—big/little, hot/cold, happy/sad

Developmental Stages for Language & Literacy: Four- & Five-Year Olds

Outside   As children develop, they begin to recognize symbols, such as letters and numbers and point out numbers and letters on signs and packages. Help them develop letter and number recognition by playing games like, "I Spy."

Inside   Children love reading the same book repeatedly. This helps them build memory, language, and literacy skills. Model reading to foster enjoyment and teach important literacy skills.

4-year-old

5-year-old

200–400+ words, sentences
Books, Rhymes, Finger Plays, Songs
- Points to parts of a book, cover, pages, words
- Objects if parents skips words/pages in a familiar book

Talking and Writing
- Is more easily understood, may mispronounce a few words
- Recites nursery rhymes, finger plays, rote counts to 20
- "Play" writes, imitates, and traces letters

Thinking and Behavior
- Names things in a category
- Shares but is self-centered, plays make-believe
- Follows a 2- to 3-part direction

Word Use
- Begins to use irregular past tense—fell (not falled)
- Compares and uses position and time words

1,500+ words, long sentences
Books, Rhymes, Finger Plays, Songs
- Has favorite books, authors, and subjects
- Recognizes most letters, a few words, and names

Talking and Writing
- Speaks clearly, fluently, with very few errors
- Knows many songs, rhymes, and a few poems
- Begins formal handwriting instruction

Thinking and Behavior
- Explains why things happen and can sequence
- Defines words by function: food—to eat, bed—to sleep
- Eager to help, expresses anger with words

Word Use
- Uses correct past tense for many verbs—ate, hid, ran

Meeting Individual Needs

Supporting English Language Learners (ELLs)

All young children need help to adjust to school, develop language skills, and learn. The English language learner needs help with all of that and with learning a new language and culture.

The beautiful thing about Pre-K is that all children, including ELLs, are acquiring the English language. Things are done differently in Pre-K for this very reason. The first step is to recognize that not all children live in homes where English is the primary language. In Pre-K, we can significantly impact children's learning with strategies to enhance a greater understanding of their world.

Every lesson throughout our *Language & Literacy Pre-K Teacher's Guide* includes a strategy that you can use with English language learners to support their learning. The strategies use hands-on experiences to promote vocabulary, understanding, and make connections between the home and school cultures. They also encourage children to speak using their new words during each activity. In addition to these strategies, you will also use multisensory experiences—music with movement, rhymes, and manipulatives.

Finally, when you work with English language learners, keep concepts or lessons in context. Allowing children to touch and see the things you discuss will be an important step in helping them understand. As your children's language develops throughout the year, reflect on their drawings and dictated writings and see their language expand and grow.

Support Strategies for All Learners

Before children can access the curriculum, they need to be able to access the daily routines of the classroom and communicate their basic needs. Your classroom may have children who need a great deal of support to get through the basics of the day for a variety of reasons, including limited English communication skills, limited home experiences, or developmental delays. Children also have varied interests, strengths, and backgrounds.

There are many strategies you will use and try throughout your teaching career. We like to focus on five strategies that are good for young children:

- **S**ocial
- **M**ultisensory
- **I**nstruction
- **L**anguage
- **E**valuation

Social: Make sure the basics are being met and that emotional well-being is addressed. Children should be able to tell an adult when they need help, are hungry, or have to go to the bathroom. They need to feel safe and comfortable first before they are ready to learn. Give extra attention to be sure children can communicate their basic needs. All children can benefit from whole group learning when it is participatory. Use song, rhyme, or repetition to engage them. Children who don't have experience will naturally follow the others.

Multisensory: Children have different learning styles: auditory, tactile, visual, kinesthetic. Many learn best from a combination of styles. Include activities where no language is required. Use tactile, kinesthetic, and visual senses in directions and activities. When possible, use manipulatives to bring concepts to life. Our multisensory approach meets the needs of diverse learning styles and levels.

Instruction: You, as the teacher, are the gateway to learning. Teach with spirit to engage children and bring meaning to learning. Children can learn from the tone of your voice, your gestures, and from interactions with others. Parents are their children's first teachers. Partnerships between parents and educators can greatly benefit student learning. Communication with parents is just as important as communication with your students. Whenever possible, use a child's experiences or background knowledge to make connections. Reach out to programs in your community that work with populations in your room. Network with school specialists.

Language: Use routines and repeated words or phrases for transitions. They have a comforting familiarity. Avoid long verbal explanations or questions by speaking in single words, short phrases, or short sentences. Speak slowly, even pausing between words. Use body language and facial expressions. Allow children to process the things you say. When you ask a question, give children ample time to process the information before you move on. Repeat lessons and activities. Young children can never get enough repetition.

Evaluation: You can use the Check for Understanding section in each activity to evaluate the need for support. Each activity includes support for children who may not be ready for the current skill. It may include a prerequisite learning step or suggest breaking instruction into smaller steps. Expect children to understand, and to have receptive language before they have expressive language. They are able to follow directions before they use words to ask and explain.

PHONOLOGICAL AWARENESS
I Hear It and Say It!

Phonological awareness is the ability to hear and manipulate parts of spoken language. Babies hear what's around them and respond to sounds, music, noises, and spoken words. Long before they know the meaning of spoken words, they respond to speech. They look toward the person speaking and recognize familiar voices. They are born imitators and effortlessly begin to imitate the environmental and speech sounds they hear.

As children develop, they begin to make sense of the words and sounds they hear. They hear spoken sounds not just as sounds running together, but as word units. They hear "timeforcake" as "time for cake." Research shows that phonological awareness is vital to reading success and is a teachable skill. Children learn to listen to and play with sounds, words, and sentences. They take them apart and put them together.

We have divided the phonological awareness domain into four (4) sub-domains: auditory or sound discrimination, rhyming, sentence and word awareness, and phonemic awareness.

Auditory Discrimination – This is the ability to recognize and distinguish noises and sounds from speech and to make sense of spoken language. Young children tell whether two sounds or two words are the same or different. When children hear that "timeforcake" is not one word, but three different words, this is auditory discrimination. They also begin to name objects that make specific sounds. ("The cow says moo.") In this skill area, children learn to:
- Identify the Sound
- Discriminate Sounds
- Discriminate Words

Rhyming – Jack and Jill went up the hill. Children learn rhyming best with nursery rhymes, songs, and poems. Rhymes can be "real" words or "nonsense" words (dat, jat, nat). Rhyming prepares them to understand the structure and patterns of language. Because rhyming is so enticing, it gets children to pay close attention to changes in sounds. It helps them to become better readers, writers, and spellers. In this skill area, children learn to:
- Recognize Rhyming Words
- Make Rhyming Words

Below is the significant research for this domain. For additional Phonological Awareness resources, see the reference section at the end of this teacher's guide.

Christie, J. F., B.J. Enz, and C. Vukelich. 2007. *Teaching Language and Literacy: Preschool through the Elementary Grades.* Boston: Pearson Education, Inc.

Lonigan, C. J., Burgess, S. R., and Anthony, J. L. 2000. "Development of Emergent Literacy and Early Reading Skills in Preschool Children: Evidence from a Latent-Variable Longitudinal Study." *Developmental Psychology* 36:596–613.

Stahl, S.A., and B.A. Murray. 1994. "Defining Phonological Awareness and Its Relationship to Early Reading." *Journal of Educational Psychology* 86(2):221–234.

PHONOLOGICAL AWARENESS
continued

Sentence and Word Awareness – This is breaking apart (segmenting) and putting together (blending) sounds in words and words in sentences. We do it with compound words (back-pack), syllables (al - li - ga - tor), onset-rime (/d/-og, /l/-og, /fr/-og), and sentences (I touch my nose). What is onset and rime? The onset is just the beginning sound of a word (everything that comes before the vowel—usually one, two, or three letters). In the word "dog," the onset is /d/. In the word frog, the onset is /fr/. The rime is also known as a word family. The rime begins with the vowel and all letters that come after it. The rime in the words "dog" and "frog" is -og. Essentially, rimes or word families have the same "last name." The last name is usually two to three letters. Common two-letter word families are: -at, -un, -ed, -an, -ar, -in, -ig, -og, -ay. When children segment an onset and rime, they are breaking apart /d/ from -og in dog. When they blend onset and rime, they are putting /d/ and -og together. Awareness of words and sentences also helps children understand that words have meaning. This allows them to play with language, tell exciting stories, and eventually, learn to read and write. In this skill area, children learn to:

- Find Words in a Sentence (Segment Sentences)
- Build Sentences with Words
- Make One Word into Two
- Make Two Words into One
- Recognize Syllables
- Divide Onset and Rime
- Combine Onset and Rime

Phonemic Awareness – Phonemic awareness and phonological awareness often are thought to be the same skill, but they are two related categories. Phonemic awareness is a more specific skill under the broad umbrella of phonological awareness. Although phonological awareness focuses broadly on the sound structure of words and sentences, phonemic awareness focuses on phonemes—the smallest units of sound. For example, recognition that "Time for cake" has three words in the sentence is phonological awareness. Recognition that the word "cake" is made up of three sounds—/k//ā//k/—is phonemic awareness. Phonemic awareness can begin in Pre-K, but is a more advanced phonological awareness skill that extends into kindergarten and early elementary school. It leads into phonics, when children attach the sounds to letters. We focus on the simplest phonemic awareness skill of isolation, the ability to identify beginning and ending sounds. In this skill area, children learn to:

- Repeat Beginning Sounds
- Identify Beginning Sound
- Identify Final Sound

Sing, Sound & Count With Me CD

The *Sing, Sound & Count With Me* CD includes 29 enjoyable songs, specifically chosen or written to reinforce key literacy and math concepts. Performed by Cathy Fink and Marcy Marxer, Grammy-winning songwriters and musicians, the CD features a variety of musical styles that capture your children's interest. Children happily sing them over and over and move to the captivating songs. The booklet included with the CD will help you with the words. Lyrics are also online at A Click Away.

You'll like it because . . .

The songs tie into activities in the *Language & Literacy Pre-K Teacher's Guide* and the *Numbers & Math Pre-K Teacher's Guide*. They introduce concepts or reinforce them, they mention the topic being taught and help children practice the skill. For example, "Syllable Sound-Off" teaches children what syllables are and helps them divide lyrics into syllables. Other songs help Pre-K children develop social-emotional skills, such as smooth transition from one activity to another, recognition of emotions, positive self esteem, or cooperation.

Where you'll see it

Phonological Awareness   Oral Language

Concepts About Print   Writing

Comprehension

Discovery Teaching in Your Day

Discovery Teaching with *Sing, Sound & Count With Me* CD

Sing, Sound & Count With Me CD entices children to sing and move to the music as it teaches important skills. The best way to use *Sing, Sound & Count With Me* is to listen to the songs and read the lyrics on your own. Then play it in the background during free play to subtly introduce it to the children. See which songs attract both you and the children. Think about how the skills fit in with your plans. Here are some ideas to help you along. The literacy activities are in **bold**.

Track–Song	Suggested Activities
1 It's Pre-K!	Swing bent arms in time. Jump two times and wave hands for chorus.
2 The Ants Go Marching	March around in groups. Hold up fingers to show numbers.
3 **I'm Happy to See You**	**Sit in a circle. Tap knees and clap with the beat.**
4 **I'm Happy to See You** (Spanish)	
5 Shape Song	Trace or hold shapes in the air. Show sides and corners.
6 Counting, Counting	Follow lyrics for movements while counting to 5.
7 **Apples and Bananas**	**Exaggerate mouth positions for sounds.**
8 **Smile**	**Make facial expressions for each verse.**
9 Counting Candles	Clap to the rhythm. Show fingers while counting.
10 **Hurry Burry**	**Make motions for each mishap.**
11 **Sing Your Name**	**Clap to the rhythm. Clap out the syllables in names.**
12 Pattern Dance	Dance and wave. Then follow lyrics for patterns.
13 **I Am a Fine Musician**	**Motion playing instruments. Clap syllables.**
14 Counting at the Table	Follow lyrics for motions, one person at a time.
15 **Dolphins Swim**	**Swim and dive following lyrics for positions.**
16 **Syllable Sound-Off**	**March around. Clap out syllables.**
17 **Inside, Outside**	**Hold index finger in front of mouth for quiet; cup hands around mouth for loud.**
18 **Tickledee-dee**	**Sway to music. Point to child when name is sung.**
19 **Leaves and Branches, Trunk and Roots**	**Wave hands, sweep down arms and body, and pat floor.**
20 Big Numbers	Point to head for know. Shake head never. Act out last line.
21 **Animals in the House**	**Look around for animals. Motion animals' actions.**
22 **That Would Be Me!**	**Make motions for fly, grow, swim, and swing.**
23 **Letters Together Make Words**	**Grasp hands together. Say with cupped hands.**
24 **Rhyming Riddles**	**Walk in a circle for chorus. Stand still and nod to beat for riddles.**
25 It's Line Up Time	Rhumba into line.
26 **Starting Sound Shuffle**	**Point to self or children for call and response.**
27 **Dumplin' Song**	**Act out question/answer with two groups. Count down with fingers.**
28 Rowboat, Rowboat	Have children play the animals and climb into the boat.
29 **Ballet Dancing Truck Driver**	**Create motion for each occupation.**

Sound Around Box™

The Sound Around Box engages children with hands-on literacy activities.
The set includes:

- Sound Around Box – Features magnetic and dry erase side panels
- Picture Tiles (42) – Promote memory, phonological awareness, and oral language
- Color Tiles (8) – Work with simple sound and syllable activities
- Activity Plates (6) – Identify the activity being presented
- Word Plate – Displays a word written by the teacher
- Magnetic Pieces for Capitals (13) – Promote alphabet knowledge
- Activity booklet – Gets you started using its 10 activities

You'll like it because . . .

The Sound Around Box holds many surprises! It gives you easy ways to teach letters, rhymes, syllables, alphabet knowledge, oral language, and more. Use this multipurpose box to build letters with the magnetic pieces for capital letters or to identify the first letter in a child's name. Fill the box with familiar items that begin with the beginning sound you are teaching. **It's a bear. Bear begins with /b/.** Use the picture tiles to match words that rhyme. Use both the color and picture tiles to break compound words into parts or identify the number of syllables. The Sound Around Box is versatile. This teacher's guide, the activity booklet, and your own great ideas will enable you and your students to get the most out of this learning tool.

Where you'll see it

Phonological Awareness

Alphabet Knowledge

Concepts About Print

Oral Language

Discovery Teaching in Your Day

Phonological Awareness

Old Favorites

Simon Says: With this game, children learn to listen carefully and practice word discrimination. To add more of a challenge, play often and pick up the pace.

Choose and Clap: Prepare a tray or box filled with familiar objects. Each child in the circle picks an object and says its name. Clap out the number of syllables in that word. Sort objects by number of syllables.

Have You Tried These?

Searching for Sounds: Take a trip around your school. Search for objects that start with a target sound, such as sandbox, slide, seeds for /s/.

Books of Rhymes: Read rhyming books for exposure. After children have listened to a rhyme a few times, let them fill in the second rhyming word. Try the same thing with songs and poems (see Book Connection on page 180 for book suggestions).

Mix in Some Get Set for School® Activities

"Tickledee-dee:" Play the song, track 18 on the *Sing, Sound & Count With Me* CD. Substitute names of different children each time you sing and have them sing the silly rhymes with their names. Continue with shapes, colors, objects, etc.

Sentence Colors: Use Sound Around Box™ Color Tiles to count the number of words in a sentence. Place one tile for each word in the sentence. Touch a tile as you say each word. Children can use counters when they are ready to count words individually.

"I Am a Fine Musician:" Play track 13 on the *Sing, Sound & Count With Me* CD. Sing the song several times with the instruments on the CD. When children know the song, substitute other instruments and clap syllables in those words.

"Sing Your Name:" Play and sing track 11 on the *Sing, Sound & Count With Me* CD. Substitute names of different children each time you sing. Clap the syllables in each name.

"Apples and Bananas:" Play track 7 on the *Sing, Sound & Count With Me* CD. After singing the song several times, ask children what sound they hear over and over in each verse.

Do You Hear What I Hear?

Identify the Sound

We hear sounds all around us. We hear sounds in the environment and sounds that are spoken. Children benefit from and enjoy identifying what makes the sounds they hear. The skill of hearing and distinguishing between sounds helps children with their speech and language abilities.

Look What We're Learning

Phonological Awareness

- Say whether a sound is an environmental sound or a speech sound
- Listen to sounds and name objects that make that sound
- Indicate when a certain sound or word is heard

Vocabulary

sounds

Do You Hear What I Hear?

Materials/Setup:
• *Sing, Sound & Count With Me* CD track 10, "Hurry Burry"

Grouping:
Small group; Whole class

English Language Learners:
Repeat the coughing heard in "Hurry Burry." Ask the child to repeat the sound. Tell the child, **I cough**, and have him repeat the phrase. Repeat with other sounds such as the clapping of hands, the stomping of feet, or humming.

Objective
Children distinguish between a variety of environmental and speech sounds.

Activity
Outside we may hear dogs barking, horns beeping, and the wind blowing. Inside we may hear doors closing, bells ringing, and people talking.

1. **Close your eyes and listen to "Hurry Burry."**

2. Play "Hurry Burry." You may want to pause after each stanza to talk about the sounds.

3. **What sounds did you hear? What made those sounds?** Have children mimic the sounds.

4. Play "Hurry Burry" again to see if the children hear new sounds that they did not hear before. Have children make motions when they hear particular sounds. For example, pretend to bang on the door.

✓ Check for Understanding

Observe children as they listen for and sing the sounds and words. Are they able to tell the difference between the words and the sounds?

Support: When children close their eyes, make a familiar sound. Ask, **What was that sound?** Perhaps: **Ah-choo** (sneeze), **meow** (cat), **ruff-ruff** (dog), knocking on a door, clapping hands, **goo-goo-ga-ga** (baby talk).

More to Learn

Guess the Sound
Have children take turns making sounds around the classroom. They can knock down some blocks, clap their hands, or make a silly sound. Have other children close their eyes and guess the sounds they hear.

Who Is It?
Divide children into two groups. Have the first group close their eyes and put their heads down on the table. Have one child in the second group say a statement. "My teacher's name is Ms. Guzman." Have the first group identify whose voice they heard.

Sound Detectives

Discriminate Sounds

Children hear sounds throughout the day. There are similarities and differences in sounds. The ability to discriminate sounds helps children with rhyming and letter sounds.

Look What We're Learning

Phonological Awareness
- Identify similarities and differences in sounds
- Indicate when a certain sound or word is heard
- Listen to sounds and name objects that make that sound

Vocabulary

same

different

© 2011 Get Set for School®

Sound Detectives

Materials/Setup:

- Animal sounds such as pig, cow, horse, dog, cat, lion, duck, chicken, monkey
- Instrument sounds such as drum, maracas, piano, guitar
- Inside sounds such as door closing, water pouring
- Outside sounds such as car, lawn mower, bus, train, airplane
- Pictures of sound sources (optional)

Grouping:
Small group; Whole class

English Language Learners:
Talk about the different sounds. Is it an everyday sound? Have children try to reproduce the sound they have heard. Make sure they use complete sentences.

Objective
Children identify sounds that are the same and sounds that are different.

Activity
Let's pretend to be detectives. A detective figures things out. Our job is to match the missing sounds.

1. **I will play a sound.** Create/play a sound from the list of sounds in the materials section. **This sound is missing its match. Let's see if we can find it.** Now create/play a second sound that doesn't match. **Is that the same sound? Sound detectives, does it match? No, those sounds are different.**

2. Create/play another set of sounds that are the same. **Were those two sounds the same? Sound detectives, do they match? Oh yes, those sounds are the same. They match. Let's do the Match Dance.**

3. Have students stand and wave their hands while turning around.

4. Continue creating/playing sounds and doing the Match Dance when appropriate. Ask children what makes the sound.

✓ Check for Understanding

Observe children as they talk about sounds that are the same and different. Can they tell if two sounds are the same? Can they identify if two sounds are different? Are they able to identify what makes a sound?

Support: As they are listening to sounds, ask children to identify what makes those sounds. **Is it an animal? Is it a machine?** Show pictures to help them determine the source. Identifying the source will help them distinguish whether the sounds are the same or different.

More to Learn

Loud and Quiet
Listen to "Inside, Outside," track 17 on the *Sing, Sound & Count With Me* CD two times. The second time, have children stand on the loud parts and sit for the quiet parts. Then have them try to sing loudly and softly with the song.

It Doesn't Belong
Play Sound Detectives and identify the sound that doesn't belong. Play two farm animal sounds and then an instrument sound. Ask the children which sound does not belong to the group.

Same & Different Words

Discriminate Words

Children are exposed to a variety of words every day. Some words are exactly alike while others sound similar, but are different. It is important to distinguish words that are the same and different to develop speech and language skills. In the long run, it increases a child's ability to spell accurately, follow directions, and improve overall reading skills.

Look What We're Learning

Phonological Awareness
- Say whether two spoken words are the same or different

Vocabulary

different

same

Same & Different Words

Materials/Setup:
- Sound Around Box™:
  - Picture Tiles featuring animals

Grouping:
Small group; Whole class

English Language Learners:
Make sure children understand same and different. Show one crayon and one book. Say, **Different**. Show two identical crayons or two identical books. Say, **Same**.

Objective
Children say whether two words are the same or different.

Activity
Let's play a game called Same or Different. Listen very carefully to hear if words sound the same or different.

1. Let's listen to animal words, **Dog . . . dog**—same. Listen, **Alligator . . . alligator**—same.

2. Let's listen to two more animal words, **Dog . . . cat**—different. Listen, **Alligator . . . mouse**—different.

3. Pass out all animal word tiles: **alligator, bear, bee, cat, dog, duck, frog, horse, mouse, ox, pig, turtle, yak.**

4. Listen carefully. I will say two animal words. You say same or different.
   Alligator . . . turtle (different)
   Dog . . . dog (same) **If you have the dog, put it on the box.**
   Bear . . . bee (different)
   Duck . . . frog (different)
   Ox . . . ox (same) **If you have the ox, put it on the box.**

5. Continue activity until all animal tiles are on the box.

✓ Check for Understanding

Observe children as they say words that are the same and different. Can they identify if two words are the same? Can they identify if two words are different?

Support: Children listen for the same name twice or for two different names. They stand up when their name is called. Say, **John . . . John.** Only John stands up. Say, **Rosa . . . Kitu.** Rosa and Kitu stand up. If two children have the same first name, add the last initial. Repeat for all names.

More to Learn

Color Words
Repeat the activity with color tiles. **Green . . . green** – same. **Green . . . red** – different.

The Odd Word
For more of a challenge, say two words that are the same and one that is different. Have children tell you the two words that are the same and/or the word that is different.

Rhyme Time

Recognize Rhyming Words

Rhyming words have the same ending sound. Young children like to say and sing words that rhyme. Rhymes teach them to recognize language patterns that will eventually help them to decode words. They also help develop vocabulary and introduce styles of writing.

Look What We're Learning

Phonological Awareness
- Say whether or not two spoken words rhyme
- Say whether two spoken words are the same or different
- Repeat rhyming words spoken by a teacher

Oral Language
- Repeat teacher's words

Vocabulary

rhyme

Rhyme Time

Materials/Setup:

- Sound Around Box™:
  - Picture Tiles featuring rhyming words: dog, log, frog, bee, key, cat, hat, green, queen, jar, car, pan, van, two, blue, yak, black

Grouping:
Small group; Whole class

English Language Learners:
Show children a toy cow and tell them, **Cow.** Then say a rhyming word for cow, such as **Wow.** Have them repeat after you at least three times, "Cow . . . Wow." Using a new object, repeat these steps, like "Book . . . Look."

Objective
Children identify rhyming words.

Activity
We are going to learn about rhyming words.

1. **Listen to the words bee and key. Say them with me. Bee . . . key. They have the same ending sound. They rhyme. Let's play Rhyme Time and find other words that rhyme.**

2. Review the Picture Tiles with the children. Place the tiles in the Sound Around Box.

3. **I want to find a tile that rhymes with bee.** Reach in the box and pull out the key tile. **Jump up if you think key rhymes with bee.**

4. Repeat with other rhyming words, but on occasion, deliberately pull out a tile that does not rhyme. **Does key rhyme with hat? No, key doesn't rhyme with hat. But key rhymes with bee.**

5. When children are ready, have them take turns choosing the tiles.

✓ Check for Understanding
Observe children jump as they hear words that rhyme. Can they tell which words rhyme and which do not?

Support: Show two tiles. **I have dog and car. I want to find a tile that rhymes with bar, far, jar, tar.** Have children point to the tile that rhymes.

More to Learn

Rhyming Animals
Play "Animals in the House," track 21 on the *Sing, Sound & Count With Me* CD. Ask questions such as, **Do goose and loose rhyme?** Mix up the animals and answers to help children discriminate rhymes.

I Can Find a Rhyme
For more of a challenge, read a book, poem, or nursery rhyme. Have children pick out rhyming words.

© 2011 Get Set for School®

Rhyme Time **37**

I Know Words That Rhyme

Make Rhyming Words

As children play with rhyme, they build vocabulary and learn sound patterns and combinations. Allow children to fill in rhyming words to build oral language skills. It is more challenging to produce rhymes than to recognize them. It is vital to be able to recognize the different beginning sounds and similar ending sounds for phonological awareness and later literacy success.

23. Letters Together Make Words
Letters together make words.
We learn new words each day.
We put the words together,
And have a new sentence to say.

Squawker can say lots of words
He helps us learn them too,
We talk about the words and then,
We know how to use them with you.
[Repeat both verses]

24. Rhyming Riddles
Chorus:
Rhyming riddles, here we go,
It's a question you might know.
Play with words—Hey, Diddle, Diddle,
Can you solve the rhyming riddle?

What drives in the street
Uses wheels and not feet?
Its name rhymes with star,
I call it a _____. [car]

What runs around parks
And makes noise when it barks?
Its name rhymes with frog,
I call it a _____. [dog]

Chorus

What falls from the sky,
Makes you wet and not dry?
Its name rhymes with plane,
I call it the _____. [rain]

Who wears a big crown
And a beautiful gown?
Her name rhymes with green,
I call her a _____. [queen]

Chorus

What has apes and bats
And big, wild cats?
Its name rhymes with blue,
I call it a _____. [zoo]

What's fun and round
And it bounces up and down
Its name rhymes with tall,
I call it a _____. [ball]

Chorus

25. It's Line Up Time
Make a line, make a line
It's line up time
[Repeat]

We need a leader in front
And a friend to get behind

And another friend gets behind [2X]
And soon we have a line
It's line up time

Hagamos una fila
Una fila, una fila
[Repetir]

Look What We're Learning

Phonological Awareness
- Produce a word that rhymes with a given word
- Say whether or not two spoken words rhyme
- Listen to songs, poems or nursery rhymes and find the rhymes

Oral Language
- Demonstrate active listening by attending to stories and instruction

Comprehension
- Listen to gain and share information

Vocabulary

riddle

I Know Words That Rhyme

Materials/Setup:

- *Sing, Sound & Count With Me* CD, track 24, "Rhyming Riddles"

- Picture Tiles from Sound Around Box™

Grouping:

Small group; Whole class

English Language Learners:

Read one page out of a rhyming picture book to children. Point out rhyming words and pictures. Have children point to and say the rhyming words and pictures.

Objective

Children say a word that rhymes with another word.

Activity

A riddle is a story with a question for us to figure out. Let's listen to "Rhyming Riddles." It's a fun song that will teach us about rhyming and riddles.

1. Play "Rhyming Riddles." Have children listen first and see when they know the riddle.

2. **Now, let's listen again and see if we can fill in the riddles.**

3. Help children fill in the missing rhyming word in each verse of the song.

4. As children improve their rhyming skills, you may want to pause at the end of each verse so that they can produce the rhyme without prompting.

5. Replay the song and have them sing along.

6. In time, hold up Picture Tiles from the Sound Around Box. Ask children to give a word that rhymes with the Picture Tile you are holding.

✓ Check for Understanding

Observe children fill in the rhyming words to "Rhyming Riddles." Do they provide a rhyming word? Do they provide a real or nonsense word to rhyme with the Picture Tile?

Support: Making up nonsense rhymes is a fun way to help teach rhyming. Have children repeat doo-blue, dellow-yellow, durple-purple, dare-square, dircle-circle, diangle-triangle.

More to Learn

Nursery Rhyme Mix

Re-create a nursery rhyme by changing some of the words to rhyming words, e.g., instead of "Humpty Dumpty sat on a wall," try "Humpty Dumpty sat on a ball."

Silly Poem

For a fun challenge, have children provide rhyming words for the following things—fox, cat, ant, and bee. Using the rhyming words, have children help you create a silly class poem, such as "Once there was a fox, he sat on a box."

Let's Break Sentences

Find Words in a Sentence

As children develop literacy skills, they learn that sentences are made of words, and words are made of sounds. In phonological awareness, we begin with spoken sentences. We start breaking (segmenting) sentences, then we practice building them. When we are done with sentences, we move on to segmenting and blending compound words.

Look What We're Learning

Phonological Awareness
- Break spoken sentences into words
- Count the number of words in a spoken sentence

Math
- Recognize that the last number said is the total

Vocabulary

word

sentence

Let's Break Sentences

Materials/Setup:
- *Sing, Sound & Count With Me* CD track 23, "Letters Together Make Words"

Grouping:
Whole class

English Language Learners:
Use a sentence that is familiar to the child. For example, "My name is Sofia." Complete the activity using that sentence.

Objective
Children break a sentence into words and count the number of words.

Activity
Today we're going to find out how words and sentences work. Let's start with a song.

1. Play "Letters Together Make Words." Have children listen to the words and then sing along.

2. **Letters together make words. Words together make sentences. Let's listen to a sentence and find out how many words it has.**

3. Have five children sit in a line. **I'm going to say a sentence. When I point at you, please stand up.** As you repeat each word of the sentence, point to one child to stand up. **I hop. I . . . hop**.

4. **How many words were in that sentence? Two words. Now let's hop!**

5. Repeat steps 3 and 4 using other action sentences such as: **I dig. I jump. I touch my nose. I reach up high. I bend my arm. I dance with my friend.**

✓ Check for Understanding

Say a sentence without pointing. Do children stand up for each word? Can they independently identify how many words are in the sentence?

Support: Lay out a bottle cap for each word in the sentence. Touch the caps as you say the sentence slowly. Have children touch each cap as they say the word. Then count the caps.

More to Learn

Look in a Book
Choose a book with simple sentences for the standing activity. Let children act out the sentence or show them an illustration for the sentences.

I Can Count Words
Add complexity by giving each child some counters to represent the words in a sentence. Use short sentences and let children select one counter per word. Count. Compare the quantities and discuss any differences.

Let's Make Sentences

Build Sentences with Words

The building of sentences with words mimics the slow pace of early reading. Children have to remember each of the words and put them together to understand meaning. It's important for them to know that words by themselves don't communicate complete thoughts. Sentences communicate full thoughts and ideas. This understanding is an important skill for language development.

Look What We're Learning

Phonological Awareness
- Build spoken words into a sentence

Oral Language
- Speak in complete sentences made up of three or more words

Vocabulary

word

sentence

Let's Make Sentences

Materials/Setup:
- Classroom objects

Grouping:
Small group (6)

English Language Learners:
Adapt this activity to help children say the individual words. Put one cap or counter on the table for each word of the sentence. As you slowly say each word, tap the corresponding cap. Have children repeat the words, tapping each cap as they go. Then have them say the complete sentence at a regular pace.

Objective
Children put a group of spoken words into a sentence.

Activity
Today we're going to build sentences.

1. **We are going to build a sentence with words, but I need your help.** Have three children line up side-by-side. Hand the third child a classroom object.

2. **Each of you say the word that I tell you.** Whisper one word in each child's ear. Say **We** to the first child, **like** to the second child, and the name of the object to the third child.

3. **Say your word when I point to you. Everyone else should listen to hear the sentence they are building.** Point to each child slowly. Make sure there's some space between words: "We . . . like . . . crayons."

4. **What sentence did they make?** (We like crayons.)

5. Repeat with other children and objects.

✓ Check for Understanding

Observe children as they listen for and build sentences. Can they say the sentence after they listen to the words?

Support: Begin this activity with two-word action sentences, such as **I hop; I wash;** or **We run.**

More to Learn

Tortoise and the Hare Sentences
Read the "Tortoise and the Hare." You be the tortoise and say a sentence very slowly. Have the children be hares and say your sentence quickly.

I Can Count My Words
Challenge children by having them make up their own sentences. They should say each word slowly, placing one counter per word. Then they can say the whole sentence quickly.

    Let's Make Sentences

Word Magic: One Word Turns into Two!

Make One Word into Two

A compound word is one word that is made from two words put together. Breaking (segmenting) compound words into two words builds vocabulary and helps children understand language. Children like to think about why the words are together, which prepares them to segment words into syllables.

Look What We're Learning

Phonological Awareness
- Break compound words apart

Oral Language
- Repeat teacher's words
- Listen to follow directions (up to 3-4 steps)

Word Magic: One Word Turns into Two!

Materials/Setup:
- Sound Around Box™
- Sunglasses
- Toothbrush
- Cupcake (toy)
- Small fishbowl
- Magic Wand
- Compound Word Picture Cards

Grouping:
Small group; Whole class

English Language Learners:
Use props when possible for the small words and for the compound word. Show a real bowl and toy fish for fishbowl.

Objective
Children separate compound words into two words.

Activity
I can turn one word into two and so can you. It's Word Magic!

1. Place the Compound Word Picture Cards into the Sound Around Box. Place items next to the box.

2. Have one child pick an item. Have him show the item to the class. **You chose sunglasses. Now drop the sunglasses into the Sound Around Box.**

3. Have a second child come forward and wave the wand over the box. Dramatically pull the correct Compound Word Picture Cards from the box.

4. Hand the Compound Word Picture Cards to the child magician and have her show them to the class. **Look! One word turned into two. Sunglasses became sun and glasses.**

5. Wave the wand again and pull out the sunglasses. **Sunglasses is made of sun and glasses. Say that with me. Sunglasses is made of sun and glasses.**

6. Repeat the magic using one of the other objects.

✓ Check for Understanding

Show the objects again. Can children say the two words that make up the compound word?

Support: Show the two Compound Word Picture Cards and the compound word object. Talk about how they are related, such as **Sunglasses are glasses we wear in the sun.**

More to Learn

Picture That
Use the Compound Word Picture Cards available on A Click Away to help segment compound words.

Give Me a Break
Say a compound word. Guide children to divide the word into two smaller words. **Cowboy is made of cow and boy.** Repeat several times. Have children choose one compound word and draw the two smaller words. Write the three words on their papers.

Two Words, New Word

Make Two Words into One

Children are amazed that they can put two words together to make a new word. Blending compound words familiarizes children with word parts and prepares them to blend syllables and sounds.

Look What We're Learning

Phonological Awareness
- Create a compound word from two familiar words

Oral Language
- Learn words linked to content being taught

Social-Emotional
- Cooperate with other children
- Take turns with peers

Two Words, New Word

Objective
Children create compound words from two familiar words.

Activity
We are going to use two words to make a new word.

1. Place two objects that make up a compound word into the box.

2. Invite two children to pull an object out of the box. Have them show their objects to the class and name them. (I have a cat.) (I have a fish.)

3. **We can make one word from these two words. Listen: cat, fish, catfish. A catfish is a real fish. Here is a picture.** Show a catfish in the fish book.

4. Repeat the activity with other objects to make these compound words: jellyfish, fishbowl, starfish, cupcake, basketball, and shoestring. Show a picture or object for each compound word.

✓ Check for Understanding

Observe children as they make compound words. Do they say the two smaller words and the compound word? Do they begin to put the words together by themselves?

Support: First segment two compound words from the list, such as starfish. Show a picture or object for the compound word. Then, break each word into two words and show the objects for those words. Blend the words back into the compound word. Say the words and have children repeat for each step.

More to Learn

Crazy Compound Words
Have fun making nonsense compound words. Put all objects for smaller words in the box. Have two children pull out objects. Guide them to say a silly compound word by putting the two words together, such as catball.

I'll Give You Half
For a challenge, give children half of a compound word, such as sun, room, or back. Have children try to give another word to make a compound word such as sunshine, bathroom, or backpack. Review the -fish words as a model.

Clap Names

Recognize Syllables

A small word part with one vowel sound is called a syllable. Children can clap and make noise to break words into syllables. Clapping emphasizes each part, or syllable. Breaking (segmenting) words into syllables prepares children to hear smaller sounds in words.

Look What We're Learning

Phonological Awareness
- Break words into syllables
- Count the number of syllables in a word (up to 4)
- Blend syllables into a complete word
- Indicate when a certain sound or word is heard

Oral Language
- Repeat teacher's words

Math
- Recognize that the last number said is the total

Vocabulary

syllable

Clap Names

Materials/Setup:
- Line It Up™:
  - Magnetic Bar
  - Coloring Cards

Grouping:
Small group; Whole class

English Language Learners:
Play and clap along with "Syllable Sound-Off," track 16 from *Sing, Sound & Count With Me* CD. Pause the song periodically to repeat syllables and clap. Where possible, point to or show pictures of the items in "Syllable Sound-Off."

Objective
Children clap and count the syllables in a word.

Activity
The small parts of a word are called syllables. Let's name pictures and clap for each word part.

1. Place the Zebra Coloring Card from Line It Up in the bar. Point to the zebra. **This is a zebra.**
2. **Listen carefully. I'm going to say and clap the syllables, ze-bra.**
3. **Now let's say and clap them together, ze-bra. Let's do it again, ze-bra.**
4. **Now let's check to see how many syllables there are in ze-bra.**
5. **There are two syllables in zebra, ze . . . bra.**
6. **Now say the word all together—zebra. Again, zebra.**
7. Repeat steps 1–6 with other Coloring Cards from Line It Up.

✓ Check for Understanding
Observe children as they say and clap the syllables. Do they clap for real syllables? Can they count the number of syllables?

Support: Make a list of your children's names by syllables. Each day feature names with different numbers of syllables.
Day 1: Feature one-syllable names. Clap and say, **Rob, Scott, Hong.**
Day 2: Feature two-syllable names. Clap and say, **E-ric, De-nise.**
Day 3: Feature three-syllable names. Clap and say, **Sa-man-tha, A-di-na.**

More to Learn

Syllable Sort
Place two Color Tiles on the Sound Around Box. Have children find Picture Tiles for two-syllable words. Touch each Color Tile as you say the syllable. Sweep over both tiles and say the whole word. Have children repeat. Try three-syllable words too.

Syllable Compare
For a challenge, give two words to children. Say and clap the syllables together. Put down a counter for each syllable. Repeat the words and say which word has more syllables by comparing the number of counters.

© 2011 Get Set for School®

Clap Names **49**

Words Have Families, Too

Divide Onset & Rime

Onset and rime are important early literacy skills. An onset is what comes before the vowel. In fish, /f/ is the onset. In frog, /fr/ is the onset. The rime is anything that follows. In fish, -ish is the rime. In frog, -og is the rime. Rimes are used to make rhymes. Rimes with the same spelling can be grouped into word families. Hat, mat, and bat have a different onset and the same rime. They belong to the -at word family.

A number of studies show that when children understand onsets and rimes, it helps them learn to read. Onsets and rimes also play a significant role in spelling.

Look What We're Learning

Phonological Awareness

- Break words into two parts: onset and rime
- Indicate when a certain sound or word is heard

Vocabulary

word family

Words Have Families, Too

Materials/Setup:
- Sound Around Box™:
  - Picture Tiles

Grouping:
Small group; Whole class

English Language Learners:
Say the name of each Picture Tile slowly. Emphasize the ending sound. Have children repeat the name of each Picture Tile. Guide children to participate without putting them on the spot.

Objective
Children group words into word families.

Activity
Change the beginning sound to make new words in a word family.

1. **People in families often have the same last name. Words can be part of a family too. This family's last name is -og.** Show the **dog** Picture Tile. **This is dog. Dog is in the -og family, dog, -og.**

2. Show the log Picture Tile. **This is log.** Show the dog tile, **dog, log. Dog** and **log** are in the **-og** family. **Let's put them together.**

3. **Let's see if there are any other words that belong to the -og family.**

4. Show and point to the Picture Tiles car and frog. **This is car. This is frog. Is car in the -og family? No, car is in the -ar family. Is frog in the -og family? Yes, frog is in the -og family.**

5. **Let's put frog with the -og family with dog and log.**

6. Repeat steps 1-5 and build word families.

✓ Check for Understanding

Have children sort Picture Tiles into word families. Observe and listen as they say the name of the tiles and group them. Do children isolate the rime?

Support: Show a Picture Tile and say the word. Say the onset as you place a Color Tile on the table. Say the rime as you place another Color Tile to the right of the first. Repeat, touching each tile as you say the parts. Then sweep your hand across both tiles and say the whole word. Have each child do the same.

More to Learn

Family Ties
Use objects that belong to the same word families. Try a baseball **bat** and a **cat**, a **pan** and a **can**, or a **pen** and a number **ten**. Have children sort objects by word families. **Hat is in the same family as bat and cat. They are in the –at family.**

United We Stand
Two children stand with arms locked. **Together you are top. Let's break top into beginning and ending sounds.** Children unlock arms. Child 1 says "/t/." Child 2 says "-op." **Repeat: /t/, -op, top.** Children lock arms and say, "Together we are top."

I Say, You Say, We Say

Combine Onset & Rime

Young children like to say and sing words that rhyme. Onset and rime teach children to recognize common sound groupings within words. When they recognize certain word endings, they can figure out unknown words and build their vocabulary.

Onset and rime apply only to one-syllable words, such as pan. The onset is everything that comes before the vowel or /p/ in pan. The rime is the rest of the word like -an in pan.

| -at | -een | -ar | -og | -ouse | -an |

Look What We're Learning

Phonological Awareness
- Blend onsets and rimes into a complete word
- Break words into two parts: onset and rime

Oral Language
- Listen to follow directions (up to 3-4 steps)

I Say, You Say, We Say

Materials/Setup:
- Sound Around Box™:
  - Pictures Tiles:
    hat, cat, queen, green,
    jar, car, frog, log, dog,
    house, mouse, pan, van

Grouping:
Small group; Whole class

English Language Learners:
Help children group the Picture Tiles into the same word family. Say the name of each Picture Tile.

Objective
Children blend onsets and rimes.

Activity
Let's have fun putting words together.

1. **Listen to me, /k/, -at. What word does that make?** (Cat) Show the Picture Tile cat. **This is a cat, /k/, -at. Your turn:** (/k/, -at.) **Now let's put the sounds together, /k/, -at, cat.**

2. **Listen to me, /h/, -at. Find the picture tile for this word. Your turn:** (/h/, -at.) **Now let's put the sounds together, /h/, -at, hat.**

3. Practice more onsets with the rime -at, such as /f/, /m/, /p/.

4. On different days, have a child pick a tile to begin.

✓ Check for Understanding

Observe and listen as children say the onsets and rimes. Do they know the onset and the rime? Can they blend them together?

Support: Help children make up fun words to help them better understand word families. **Let's make words in the -og family. I say the first sound and you say the ending, -og. Then let's say it together, d . . .** Children say, "og." Everyone says, **dog**. Repeat using other consonants. Use an alphabet chart for reference. Have fun using nonsense words too.

More to Learn

Matching Rimes
Place three Picture Tiles on the Sound Around Box. Two of the three tiles should have matching ending sounds. Have children identify which ending sounds match. Say the onset, rime, and whole word for each tile.

Match the End
Use Sound Around Box Picture Tiles to play Memory Match. Place all tiles face up. Have children take turns picking two tiles with the same ending sounds. Guide them to say the onset, rime, and whole word for each tile. Let the child keep matching tiles.

In the Beginning

Repeat Beginning Sounds

Alliteration is the repeated use of the same sound at the beginning of words. Poetry and nursery rhymes that use alliteration make it fun and easy to notice beginning sounds.

Read alliterative poems and nursery rhymes regularly before you start to work with beginning sounds. You will find that children are better prepared to identify the first sound in spoken words. They will continue this initial step toward reading in kindergarten.

Nursery Rhymes: Little Tommy Tittlemouse, Peter, Peter Pumpkin Eater, Wee Willie Winkie
Tongue Twisters: Betty Botter, Peter Piper, She Sells Seashells
Finger Plays: Five Little Peas, Tommy Thumb

Look What We're Learning

Phonological Awareness
- Identify the repeated initial sound in words and sentences
- Identify the first sound in a spoken word

Vocabulary

beginning

Materials/Setup:
No materials required

Grouping:
Whole class

English Language Learners:
Make sure children understand what it means to repeat something. Have them repeat something you say. Then have them repeat an action. You can also use "Peter Piper" to demonstrate the repetition of the initial /p/ sound. Repeat the /p/ sound in each word by saying **/p/ /p/ /p/ /p/ Peter, /p/ /p/ /p/ /p/ Piper.**

Objective
Children identify the initial sound in words.

Activity
Let's make silly words that start with the same sound.

1. Sit in a circle. Make sure the child sitting to your right has a name that starts with a sound that others can hear and say easily (/m/, /t/, /p/, /d/, /s/).

2. **Monica's name starts with /m/. I'm going to make all of your names start with /m/.**

3. Say each child's name, substituting /**m**/ for the initial sound. For names that start with vowels, just add the initial sound. **Monica, Mill** (Will), **Mailey** (Bailey), **Mate** (Kate), **Mantonio** (Antonio) **. . . What sound was at the beginning of all our names? Yes, /m/ was at the beginning of our names.**

4. Children may join you when they understand. If not, invite them to try when they are ready.

5. Repeat with the next student in the circle. Save difficult starting sounds to the middle or end of the activity if you can (/w/, /r/, /l/, /kw/, /ch/, /sh/).

✓ Check for Understanding

Observe children as they say the silly names. Can they say the starting sound? Can they substitute the starting sound in names?

Support: Introduce every alliterative nursery rhyme by repeating the alliterative sound. /p/ /p/ /p/ . . . Peter, Peter Pumpkin Eater.

More to Learn

Starting Sound Shuffle
Play "Starting Sound Shuffle" from *Sing, Sound & Count With Me*, track 26. Repeat each line and make the motions described in the song.

Tongue Twister Twist
Have children say words that begin with the same sound. Write the words on the board. Create a silly alliterative sentence using their words. You can also substitute the words into an existing rhyme, e.g., Patti Piper pet a peck of purple puppies.

How Does It Begin?

Identify Beginning Sound

Young children love to hear and say the sounds in words. Pictures help them focus on words. As they say the words for the pictures slowly, they can listen for the beginning sounds. When children understand beginning letter sounds, they can eventually attach sounds to letters and read words.

Look What We're Learning

Phonological Awareness
- Identify the first sound in a spoken word
- Name words that start with the same sound

Comprehension
- Listen to perform a task

How Does It Begin?

Materials/Setup:
- Line It Up™:
  - Magnetic Bar
  - Letter Cards
    B, C, D, M, S, T

Grouping:
Small group; Whole class

English Language Learners:
Make sure children understand first/beginning. Have children stand in a line. Ask them to identify the child standing first in line. Have them shift in line and state the name of the new person at the beginning of the line. Note: The Spanish word for first is *primer* (pronounced *pree-mair*).

Objective
Children identify beginning letter sounds.

Activity
Listen to bat. The first sound in bat is /b/. Let's find more words that begin with /b/.

1. Using Line It Up, place the picture side of the B Letter Card in the bar.

2. **Let's name these pictures.** Start saying each word slowly to emphasize the first sound.

3. **I am listening for words that begin with /b/. Does boots begin with /b/? /b/ -oots. Yes, boots begins with /b/.** Repeat for each picture.

4. Use other Line It Up Letter Cards for more beginning sounds.

✓ Check for Understanding
Observe children as they identify the beginning sound of a word. Can they identify words with the same or different beginning sounds?

Support: Show two Sound Around Box™ Picture Tiles that begin with the same sound. Introduce each tile by repeating the beginning sound before saying the word: /b/ /b/ /b/ . . . boots, /b/ /b/ /b/ . . . banana.

More to Learn

The Real Deal
Point out and name real objects in the classroom. **Here is a desk. Listen: desk. Raise your hand if you hear /d/ at the beginning of desk.** After a few tries, have children say the sound if they know it.

Look in a Book
For more of a challenge, give each child a picture book. Hold up a Sound Around Box Picture Tile. Say the word and identify the beginning sound. Have children look at the pictures in their books to see if they can find one that begins with the same sound as the tile.

The End

Identify Final Sound

We teach ending sounds in this order: rhyming words, onset rime, and final sounds. Rhymes are words of any length or spelling with the same ending sound (afternoon/June). Rimes are ending sounds in one syllable, onset rime words (dog, frog). Final sounds are the smallest ending sounds or phonemes. Words do not have to rhyme to have the same final sound (pen, tan). Identifying beginning and ending sounds in words prepares children for reading.

Look What We're Learning

Phonological Awareness
- Identify the ending sound in a spoken word
- Indicate when a certain sound or word is heard

Materials/Setup:
- Sound Around Box™:
  - Picture Tiles

Grouping:
Small group; Whole class

English Language Learners:
Make sure children understand last/ending. Have them stand in a line. Ask them to identify the child standing last in line. Have them shift in line and state the name of the new person at the end of the line. Note: The Spanish word for last is *final* (pronounced *fee-naahl*).

Objective
Children identify ending sounds in words.

Activity
Let's talk about the sounds we hear at the end of words.

1. Show bus Picture Tile. **This is a bussss. Bus ends with /s/.** Stretch out the /s/ sound while pretending to stretch a rubber band. **Let's stretch bus with our pretend rubber bands. Bussssssss.**

2. Show horse Picture Tile. **This is a horsssse. Horsssse ends with /s/. Let's stretch horse with our rubber bands. Horsssssssse.**

3. Show mouse picture tile. **This is a moussssse. Let's stretch moussssssse.**

4. **What ending sound did you hear? /s/ just like bussss and horsssse.**

5. Repeat with Picture Tiles of other matching ending sounds.

✓ Check for Understanding

Listen to queen and pan. Let's stretch out the ending sounds. What sound do they end with? Listen and observe the children as they stretch out the words. Are children able to identify the ending sounds?

Support: Some ending sounds are easier for children to hear than others. Try hard stopping sounds first, /k/, /d/, /g/, /p/, /t/.

More to Learn

Sound Stretch
Use classroom objects that have the same ending sound to do the activity. Children can hold objects while they stretch out the sounds.

Matching Sounds
For a challenge, place three Picture Tiles on the side of the Sound Around Box. Two of the three Picture Tiles should have matching ending sounds. Have the children stretch out the words and identify which ending sounds match.

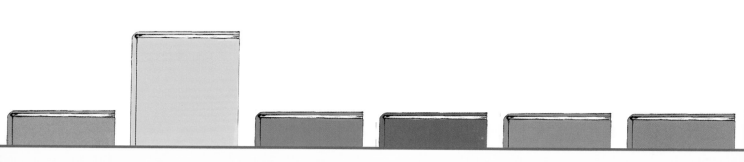

ALPHABET KNOWLEDGE
Letters, Letters, Letters

The ABCs are the building blocks of the English language. We need these letters to speak, read, and write. We put letters together to make words, words together to make sentences, and sentences together to tell stories. We also need letters to read our favorite books and to write stories and poetry. Alphabet knowledge is the ability to name the letters of the alphabet and recognize the letters in print.

Research tells us that recognizing the alphabet is one of the most accurate predictors of early reading success (Johnston, 2004). In Pre-K, you will have a wide range of alphabet recognition in your classroom. Some children will be able to sing the whole alphabet, while some may only know the first letter in their name. Activities in this section recognize the differences found in each classroom. We believe that children learn their letters through singing, building, and matching. Whether children are practicing letters that they already know or learning their letters for the first time, they will enjoy these Get Set for School® products and activities.

The activities in this domain help children learn to:
- **Distinguish Letters from Pictures**
- **Recognize Letters**
- **Position Letters**
- **Recognize Letters in Name**
- **Identify Letters in Name**
- **Identify Capital Letters**
- **Identify Lowercase Letters**
- **Match Capital and Lowercase Letters**

Below is the research for this domain. For additional Alphabet Knowledge resources, see the reference section at the end of this teacher's guide.

Bloodgood, J. W. 1999. "What's in a Name? Children's Name Writing and Literacy Acquisition." *Reading Research Quarterly* 34(3): 342-367.

Chall, J. 1996. *Learning to Read: The Great Debate*. New York: McGraw-Hill.

Johnston, F. R. 2004. "Phonics, phonological awareness, and the alphabet." *EPS Update,* April. http://eps.schoolspecialty.com/downloads/articles/phonological_awareness.pdf

Line It Up™

Line It Up Letter Cards engage children with hands-on activities that foster early literacy and motor skills. The Line It Up Letter Cards set includes:

- 26 Letter Cards
  - Crayon stroke to trace letters
  - Colorful pictures to name on picture side
- Activity booklet
  - Get started with activities in this booklet. There are lessons for every letter.
- Line It Up Bar
  - Unique display bar holds cards in place while allowing children to place cards in, out, and around the bar

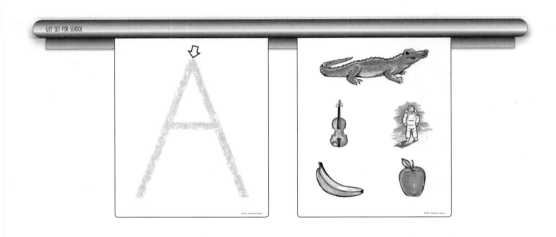

You'll like them because . . .

Line It Up Letter Cards help you introduce letter formation and letter recognition. They also encourage good writing habits. The crayon stroke Letter Cards fit into a bar to create a vertical writing surface. This promotes good wrist position and helps children build strength in the shoulders and arms. On the back of the Letter Cards are colorful pictures that expose children to phonological awareness skills. Children will say and clap syllables and identify pictures that have the same beginning sound. Use activities in this teacher's guide, the activity booklet, or create your own great ideas to make the most of the Line It Up Letter Cards.

Where you'll see them

Alphabet Knowledge   **Concepts About Print**

Discovery Teaching in Your Day

Alphabet Knowledge — Capital Letters

Old Favorites

Alphabet Read and Sing: Use alphabet books to introduce new letters. Put a special bookmark or paperclip on the page with the letter you want to introduce. Turn the pages of the book to show letters as the children sing the alphabet. Stop at the special marker and introduce the target letter. (See Book Connection on page 181 for book suggestions.)

Alphabet Cereal: Show children a large capital letter. Give each student a cup of alphabet cereal. Have them dump the cereal on the table and search for the target letter.

Sensory Letters: Practice writing letters with different kinds of materials. Fill a shallow pan with shaving cream or just spread it on a table. Then model writing letters with your child. Take turns to write letters or write letters in a name. Many other materials are suitable for this activity: sand, flour, sugar, finger paint, liquid soap, rice.

Have You Tried These?

Sun Letters: Cut out the first letter in a child's name and place it on a piece of construction paper. Set the letters in the sun. Remove letters and laminate all pieces. Have children match the letter from their name to the sun-bleached letters on the construction paper.

Letter Path: Write capital letters on construction paper. Create a letter path to something fun, e.g., centers, playground, snack time. Children must name each letter to move along the path. This can be done individually or in small groups.

Mix in Some Get Set for School® Activities

Capitals with Capital Letter Cards and Wood Pieces: Use Capital Letter Cards and Wood Pieces to build capitals. Point to a Capital Letter Card. **This is F. F starts at the** ☺. Describe each step as you place the Wood Pieces on the card. **I'm getting a Big Line to start F. I'm putting the Big Line right here, under the** ☺. **Now, I'm getting a Little Line to put at the top. Now, I'm getting another Little Line to put in the middle. I made F.** Remove the pieces and have the child build the letter. When child is ready, build the letters together using blue Mats.

Roll-A-Dough Letters®: Use Roll-A-Dough Letters to form capitals out of dough. Place a Tray Card in the tray. Show children how to roll dough and cut it to size. Place dough pieces on the card to form the letter. Have children imitate.

Sign In Please!: Preschoolers develop many important skills by learning to sign-in alphabetically. Prepare a blackboard or dry erase board with a wide stop line near the bottom. Write **A** up high, but within children's reach. Ask, **Whose name begins with A? Adam!** Adam comes to the board and signs in by making a Big Line down from **A**. He stops on the line. Continue with **B**. Children can also circle and underline letters.

Slate Letters: Children learn about capital letters by tracing them with small tools on a Slate. Use small sponges and chalk to help children learn our special technique known as Wet-Dry-Try. With this multisensory strategy, children learn proper letter formations and correct orientation.

A-B-C Touch & Flip® Cards

A-B-C Touch & Flip Cards engage Pre-K children with hands-on activities. The set includes:

- 27 Picture Cards
  - Alphabetical animal puzzle for easy ABC order
  - Three different background colors for sorting alphabet—beginning, middle, and end
  - Capitals with textured surface to trace on one side
- 26 Letter Cards
  - Capitals to match on one side
  - Lowercase letters to match on the other side
- A smiley face ☺ in the top left corner helps children know that a card is right-side up.
- Activity booklet

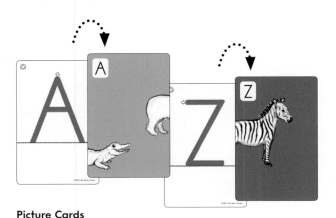

Picture Cards

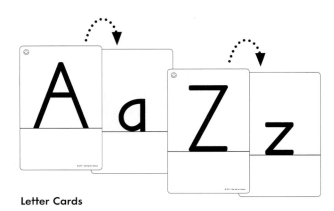

Letter Cards

You'll like them because . . .

A-B-C Touch & Flip Cards are easy to use. They reinforce good capital letter formation, enable capital and lowercase letter recognition, and promote letter memory. Children can learn letter names, match capital and lowercase letters, and complete an animal alphabet puzzle. You can use them for whole class or center-based activities. Children can self-check their work as they put the animals together or pair capital to lowercase letters. Use activities in this teacher's guide, the activity booklet, or create your own exercises to make the most of the A-B-C Touch & Flip Cards.

Where you'll see them

Alphabet Knowledge   **Concepts About Print**

Discovery Teaching in Your Day

Alphabet Knowledge — Lowercase Letters

Old Favorites

Point and Sing: This is an old-time favorite. Simply place a letter poster at eye level, and together point and sing the ABCs.

I Spy: Instead of searching for capitals, challenge children to search for letters they see in lowercase.

It's in the Book: Give each child an A-B-C Touch & Flip® Letter Card and short picture book. Have children explore their books and find matches for their letters in the text. They can match lowercase, capitals, or both. For added fun, give each child a cup. Put in a penny or counter for each match found.

Have You Tried These?

A Letter Book: Children find lowercase letters in magazines and newspapers. Encourage them to paste the letters they find in a personal Letter Book. Children can add letter stickers and stamps to the pages. At the end of the year, send the book home for children to practice over the summer. This book also teaches that a letter can look many different ways and still be the same letter.

Letter Path: Write lowercase letters on construction paper. Create a letter path to something fun, e.g., centers, playground, snack time. Children must name each letter to move along the path. This can be done individually or in small groups.

Letters in Names: Have children hold name cards (in title case). When you introduce a lowercase letter, have children whose names begin with that letter show the capital at the beginning of their names. Then have children with the letter within their names show the lowercase letter. Write both on the board.

Mix in Some Get Set for School® Activities

Letter Hunt: Give each child an A-B-C Touch & Flip Letter Card. Have children explore the room and find matches for their letters on classroom objects. They can match capitals, lowercase letters, or both. For more excitement, give each child a cup. Add a penny or counter to the cup for every match found.

Capital Partners: The easiest lowercase letters to recognize look just like their capital partners. When it's time for children to recognize lowercase letters, teach letters **c**, **o**, **s**, **v**, **w** first. The song, "CAPITALS & Lowercase," on our *Rock, Rap, Tap & Learn* CD will help you teach this.

Match and Reveal: Use A-B-C Touch & Flip Cards to match capitals side by side. Then flip each Letter Card to show the lowercase letter, leaving the Animal Card capital next to it.

Blackboard with Double Lines: Children learn lowercase letters by tracing them with small tools on a large board. Use small sponges and chalk to help them learn our Wet-Dry-Try technique. This multisensory strategy teaches proper letter formations and correct orientation every time.

Fishing for Letters

Distinguish Letters from Pictures

Pictures, letters, and symbols are all around us and have meaning. Children may be able to recognize that a stop sign is red, but don't know that it is an octagon and has letters that spell STOP. It is important that children can distinguish among pictures, letters, and symbols, because this is an early skill in recognizing meaning in their environment.

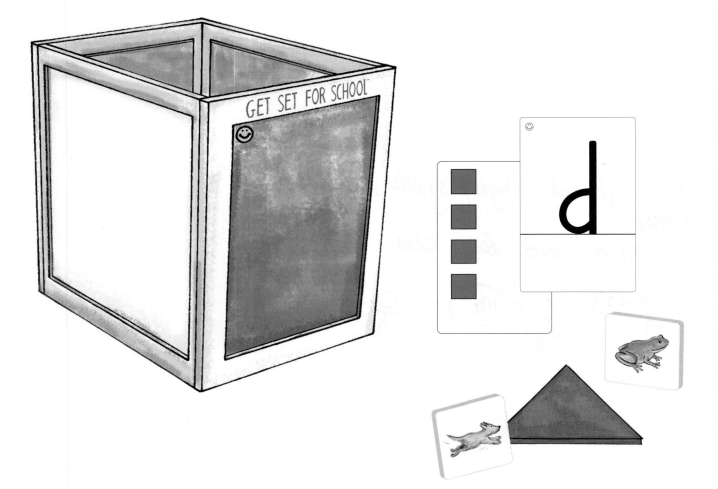

Look What We're Learning

Alphabet Knowledge
- Distinguish between letters, pictures, and other symbols
- Point to and name capital letters

Social-Emotional
- Imitate teacher's body movements
- Participate in imaginary and dramatic play

Sensory Motor
- Notice and attach meaning to visual information

Vocabulary

letter
number
picture
shape

Fishing for Letters

Materials/Setup:
- Sound Around Box™:
  - Picture Tiles
- A-B-C Touch & Flip® Cards
- 1-2-3 Touch & Flip® Cards
- Mix & Make Shapes™
- Bucket for letters

Grouping:
Small group; Whole class

English Language Learners:
Show an **A** from the A-B-C Touch & Flip Cards. **This is a letter.** Show the other side. **This is a picture.** Continue with other cards and have children tell you if you are showing a letter or a picture.

Objective
Children distinguish between letters and pictures or other symbols.

Activity
We are going fishing for letters.

1. Place A-B-C Touch & Flip Cards, 1-2-3 Touch & Flip Cards, Picture Tiles, and Mix & Make Shapes in the Sound Around Box.

2. Demonstrate fishing. Take out a letter. **Look, I caught a B. B is a letter. I will put it in our letter bucket.** Throw anything that isn't a letter back in the box.

3. Let children take turns fishing. Help children talk about and sort what they have caught. **What did you catch? Is it a letter? Picture? Shape? Number?**

✓ Check for Understanding
Observe children as they go fishing. Can they distinguish between a letter, picture, or symbol?

Support: Use A-B-C Touch & Flip Cards and the 1-2-3 Touch & Flip Cards. Mix up Letter and Number Cards. Have children help you name them and say the letter or number. **This is E. E is a letter. It goes in the letter pile. This is 3. 3 is a number. It goes in the number pile.**

More to Learn

Sort Yourself
Hand out letters, numbers, shapes, and pictures to children so that each child has one item. Identify an area in the room for each category. Help children sort and group themselves by category.

Signs All Around
For a challenge, print common signs like a stop sign, yield sign, speed limit sign, no swimming sign, etc. Help children identify the different shapes, letters, numbers, and pictures in each sign.

Sing & Point with Me

Recognize Letters

Singing the ABCs is an important first step in learning letters. Children can sing the "Alphabet Song" before they can recognize or name letters. When they can sing the song as they look at an alphabet display, they can connect the letter names to the symbols.

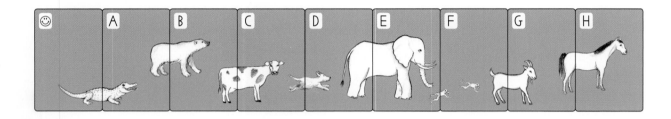

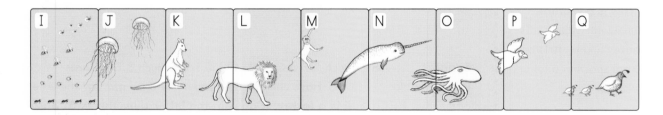

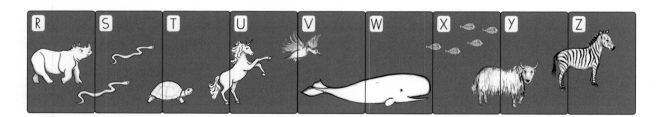

Look What We're Learning

Alphabet Knowledge
- Point to and name capital letters
- Point to and name lowercase letters

Vocabulary

alphabet

Sing & Point with Me

Materials/Setup:
- A-B-C Touch & Flip® Picture Cards

Grouping:
Whole class

English Language Learners:
Have children listen to and sing along as you sing the "Alphabet Song" slowly. Have children point to and sing the letters with you.

Objective
Children recognize and name capital and lowercase letters.

Activity
Let's have fun singing the ABCs.

1. Use three tables. Put green Picture Cards on Table 1, yellow on Table 2, and blue at Table 3.

2. Divide class into three table groups. Children at tables put the Picture Card puzzle together. Assign tables by children's first initials: green A–H, yellow I–P, blue Q–Z.

3. When the Picture Cards are together, everyone sings while looking at the cards on each table. Flip and show each card for the children as the class sings the letter. You'll need to lead the class to sing slowly so you can keep up with the flipping.

4. Sing the song again, pointing to each letter as you sing.

✓ Check for Understanding

Observe children singing. Can children name letters in alphabetical order as you point to the letters?

Support: Sing the "Alphabet Song," track 2 on the *Get Set for School Sing Along* CD. Have children touch the A-B-C Touch & Flip Cards as they sing.

More to Learn

Silly Singing ABCs
You and children alternate singing letters of the alphabet. You and children point to the letters as they sing. You sing A, children sing B. You sing C, children sing D.

Letter Leaders
Choose one leader for each table. Sing "Alphabet Song" and have the leader point as everyone sings.

Letters Up!

Position Letters

As children transition from the world of real objects to the world of symbols—letters and numbers—they need to be taught that letters and numbers only make sense if they are placed right-side up. Proper letter orientation prepares them to recognize letters and succeed as they start to write letters.

Look What We're Learning

Alphabet Knowledge
- Position capitals right-side up
- Point to and name capital letters

Sensory Motor
- Use fingers to open and close fasteners, hold cards
- Attach meaning to visual information

Vocabulary

capital

Letters Up!

Materials/Setup:
- Line It Up™:
  - Magnetic Bar
  - Letter Cards
- Dry erase crayons

Grouping:
Small group; Whole class

English Language Learners:
Discuss letters one-on-one using the A-B-C Touch & Flip® Cards. Help children to finger trace. Say the letter parts out loud as children trace with their fingers.

Objective
Children place capitals right-side up and learn proper letter formation.

Activity
I have a lot of letters. Let's hang up letters today and see if we can place them correctly.

1. Place Letter Cards on the floor.
2. Have one child choose a letter. **Can you name your letter? That's right, it's the letter R. Let's hang up the letter so our friends can see.**
3. Help child to hang letter on Line It Up Bar. **The yellow stripe goes at the top. That means the letter is right-side up.**
4. **We can finger trace the letter or trace it with a crayon. Which one do you want to do?**
5. Model the proper letter formation and then give child a turn.
6. Repeat with other letters.

✓ Check for Understanding
Notice if children naturally turn Letter Cards to be vertical and right-side up.

Support: You and a child take turns pointing out the starting icon and naming the letter on the Line It Up Letter Cards.

More to Learn

Smiley Face Helper
Show children the smiley face in the top left corner of the A-B-C Touch & Flip Cards. Children trace the letter two to three times with their finger and then name the letter.

Are They Right?
Give children the green, yellow, or blue set of cards from A-B-C Touch & Flip Cards. Have children put the animal puzzle together and turn over the cards to check that the letters are right-side up.

Please Pass L

Recognize Letters in Name

Children's names are special to them and they quickly learn to recognize letters in their own names. What better way to learn capital letters than to use something as important as their own names!

Look What We're Learning

Alphabet Knowledge
- Recognize and name letters in own first and last name

Oral Language
- Use manners in conversation

Social-Emotional
- Take turns

Vocabulary

capital
first
beginning

Materials/Setup:
- Line It Up™ Letter Cards
- A-B-C Touch & Flip® Cards (if you need additional Letter Cards)

Grouping:
Whole class

English Language Learners:
In the activity, use shorter sentences for children to repeat, **L is for Luis.** Have everyone repeat as you pass the letter, "L is for Luis." Have Luis repeat after everyone, "L is for Luis."

Objective
Children recognize capital letters in their own names while they practice manners.

Activity
We all have a very special letter. It's the letter that starts your name. I'm going to pass your special letter to each of you.

1. Children sit in a circle.
2. Give L card to the nearest child. **This is L for Liam. Please pass it on.**
3. Help children say the letter as they pass it on.
4. When Liam gets **L**, he says, "Thank you. I got **L** for Liam."
5. Repeat with other letters.

✓ Check for Understanding
Observe children as they say and pass the letter. Do they know the name of the letter? Do they know whose name starts with the letter?

Support: Give children the A-B-C Touch & Flip Cards that start their names. Have them say the letter, finger trace the letter, and say their name. **L is for Liam.**

More to Learn

Capital Call Out
Give each child the first letter of their first name. Call out a child's name, **Liam.** Liam holds up his card. **What letter is Liam holding? L. L is for Liam.** Have everyone repeat, "L is for Liam."

Sing and Pop
Sing the "Alphabet Song" slowly. Point to the letter wall cards or poster as you sing. Have children pop up when they see and hear the first letter of their names.

That's My Letter

Identify Letters in Name

Children recognize letters in things that have meaning to them. They like to learn the letters in their own names and in their friends' names. Names are a great way to teach letter recognition and positioning.

Note: The Sound Around Box™ is backwards so you can see it in this picture. In the classroom, the blue side with the Magnetic Pieces for Capitals should face the children.

Look What We're Learning

Alphabet Knowledge
- Recognize and name letters in own first and last name
- Position capitals right-side up

Vocabulary

capital
first
beginning

That's My Letter

Materials/Setup:

- Sound Around Box™:
  - Activity Plate for Name
  - Magnetic Pieces for Capitals
- Wood Pieces for Capital Letters
- Blue Mat – one per child
- Dry erase marker
- Wood Pieces Letter Chart (if needed)

Grouping:

Small group; Whole class

English Language Learners:

Have children assemble the Animal Puzzle with the A-B-C Touch & Flip® Cards. After the puzzle is completed, flip each card to show the larger letter. Name letters as you flip.

Objective

Children recognize capital letters in their own names and practice positioning letters right-side up by building the first letter of their names.

Activity

We all have a special letter. It is the first letter in our names. Let's see which letter we will make.

1. Children sit on the floor, each child with a blue Mat.

2. Select the correct Magnetic Piece from inside the Sound Around Box. **I have a Big Line.** Place the piece correctly on the blue side of the box.

3. Children choose the same Wood Piece and imitate teacher on Mat.

4. Repeat 2 and 3 using the correct pieces in sequence until the letter is finished.

5. **Stand up if your name starts with this letter.** Write the children's names on white side of the box.

6. Repeat with other letters.

✓ Check for Understanding

Observe children building letters correctly on their Mats and see if they stand when their letters are made. Do children position the letters right-side up? Do children know the first letter in their names?

Support: Model letters on a Mat sitting beside the child.

More to Learn

Roll a Letter

To vary the lesson, use Roll-A-Dough Letters® instead of Wood Pieces.

Last Names

Challenge students by using the first letter of their last names instead of their first names.

Letter Tags

Identify Letters in Name

Young children should recognize letters in their names in both capitals and in title case. When they can match letters to a name card, they can learn name recognition and letter sequence.

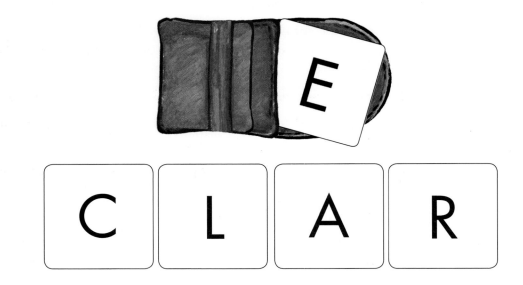

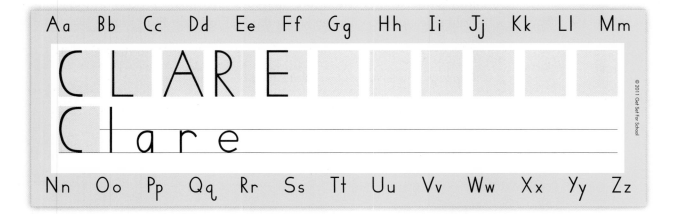

Look What We're Learning

Alphabet Knowledge
- Recognize and name letters in own first and last name
- Point to and name capital letters

Sensory Motor
- Attach meaning to visual information
- Use index finger to trace letters
- Use fingers to hold cards

Letter Tags

Materials/Setup:
- Tag Bags® (one per child)
- Capital and Lowercase Letter Tags (printed on cardstock)

- Name Cards

Grouping:
Small group

English Language Learners:
Have children say the letters of each child's name as they are shown.

Objective
Children recognize letters in their own names and practice positioning letters in correct sequence.

Activity
Inside these little Tag Bags are special tags. We will build our names with our Letter Tags. They are the letters in your name.

1. Prepare a Tag Bag for each of the children containing the letters of their names.

2. Give children the Tag Bags with the letters of their names in the pocket.

3. Give children Name Cards with their names printed on them.

4. Children open the Tag Bag and find what's in the pocket. **What's in the pocket?**

5. Children remove the Letter Tags and build their names following the model on their Name Cards.

6. Help children say the letters in their names.

7. When children are ready, repeat the activity with names in title case.

✓ Check for Understanding

Observe children as they match their tags to the Name Cards. Are they able to build their names? Can they say the letters in their names?

Support: As children open their Tag Bags, have them find the first letter in their names. Help them say the letters and build their names.

More to Learn

Last Names Too
Repeat activity using each child's last name.

Names in Our Class
To challenge the class, put Name Cards in Tag Bags. Have children open a Tag Bag and match the name on the card with the right person in the class. Guide them as needed.

Letter Time

Identify Capital Letters

Children love show and tell. When they bring items from home to help teach the letter of the day, it sparks their interest. They will see that their show-and-tell items have something in common—capital letters.

Look What We're Learning

Alphabet Knowledge
- Point to and name capital letters

Social-Emotional
- Take turns

Sensory Motor
- Move an object in one hand to position it for use

Vocabulary

capital

Letter Time

Materials/Setup:
- Sound Around Box™:
  - Magnetic Pieces for Capitals
- Objects from home
- Dry erase marker
- Letter Time Note to Home

Grouping:
Small group; Whole class

English Language Learners:
Repeat the names of items one at a time as they are removed from the box. Have children repeat after you.

Objective
Children recognize and name capital letters.

Activity
Let's look in our box and see the letter B things we brought from home.

1. Build **B** with Magnetic Pieces on the Sound Around Box.
2. Have a child remove the first item from the box. **Look, we have a bear. Bear starts with B.**
3. Write **BEAR** on the side of the Sound Around Box. Point to the **B** in **BEAR**. **Bear starts with B.**
4. **Who brought the bear?** Thank you for bringing your **bear.**
5. Repeat steps 2-4.
6. After all items are listed ask, **How are all of these things alike? Yes, they all start with B.**

✓ Check for Understanding

Observe children as they participate. Can they point to and name the letter? Do they understand what the items have in common?

Support: Repeat the names of items as they are removed from the box. Be sure to say, **Bear starts with B.**

More to Learn

Letter Hunt
Have children hunt around the room for the capital letter of the day. When they see the letter, have them point it out to you. Talk about the item that has the letter of the day.

Capital Letter Sort
Use blank Word Time™ cards to write words beginning with capital letters. Have children sort the words by beginning letter.

Lowercase Limbo

Identify Lowercase Letters

Lowercase letters are everywhere. Children find lowercase letters on traffic signs, on classroom posters, and in their books. When children recognize and name lowercase letters, they are ready to take another step toward learning how to read and write.

Look What We're Learning

Alphabet Knowledge
- Point to and name lowercase letters

Social-Emotional
- Take turns

Sensory Motor
- Play with body awareness, balance, and regard for people and equipment

Vocabulary

lowercase

match

Lowercase Limbo

Materials/Setup:
- A-B-C Touch & Flip® Cards (lowercase)
- Long ribbon for limbo
- *Get Set for School Sing Along* CD, track 2, "Alphabet Song"
- Pre-K Wall Cards

Grouping:
Small group; Whole class

English Language Learners:
Give students pairs of objects such as different socks. Have children find the matching socks and say "These socks match." Find opportunities to have them match throughout the day in different contexts.

Objective
Children recognize and name lowercase letters.

Activity
Do we know our ABCs? Let's check!

1. Listen to the "Alphabet Song." With a poster or Pre-K Wall Cards, sing and point to the alphabet. Continue the music quietly in the background.

2. Pass out lowercase A-B-C Touch & Flip Cards that look similar to their capital matches: **c, o, p, s, v, w, x, z.**

3. Model with another child how to hold the ribbon for limbo.

4. Call out a letter. **If you have the letter o, hold it up. Come do the limbo!** Child with o walks under the ribbon.

5. **What letter did the limbo?** (o)

✓ Check for Understanding

Observe children as they play Lowercase Limbo. Do the children hold up the correct letter? Do they name the letter correctly?

Support: Introduce only two to three letters at a time. Make sure children recognize these letters before adding more.

More to Learn

Lowercase Letter Laugh
Give each child a lowercase letter from the A-B-C Touch & Flip Cards. Call out the letter. Have a child hold up the letter and say the letter in a silly voice. Have the other children repeat in the same silly voice.

Lowercase Look & See
Place Word Cards from Word Time™ on the floor. Give each child a lowercase letter from the A-B-C Touch & Flip Cards. Have them find words that begin with their letters.

Letter Friends

Match Capital & Lowercase Letters

When children recognize capital and lowercase letters, they begin to unlock print in the world around them. Children like to match colors, shapes, and socks, as well as capital and lowercase letters.

Look What We're Learning

Alphabet Knowledge
- Match all capital and lowercase letters

Social-Emotional
- Cooperate with other children

Sensory Motor
- Naturally move and place body to perform tasks

Vocabulary

match

Materials/Setup:
- A-B-C Touch & Flip® Cards

Grouping:
Small group; Whole class

English Language Learners:
Model using complete sentences when naming capitals and lowercase letters. **This is capital D. This is lowercase d.** Have entire class repeat the complete sentence.

Objective
Children match letters, capital to capital, and capital to lowercase.

Activity
Some of you have a capital letter. Some of you have a lowercase letter. Find your matching letter friend.

1. Give each child one A-B-C Touch & Flip Card. Half of the children should get a capital letter and the other half should get the matching lowercase letter. For the beginning of the year, start with capital and lowercase letters that look alike: **C, O, P, S, V, W, X, Z.**

2. **Find your matching letter friend. Sit down together.**

3. **Where are C letter friends? Stand and hold up your cards.**

4. Have all the children say the letters. This is capital C and this is lowercase c.

5. Repeat for other letters.

✓ Check for Understanding
Observe children as they find their match. Can they match capital letters to lowercase letters? Can they name the letters?

Support: Use fewer A-B-C Touch & Flip Cards. Prompt children to check both sides of their cards.

More to Learn

Letter Marks the Spot
Place Line It Up™ Letter Cards around the room. Hand out A-B-C Touch & Flip Cards (lowercase side). Have children stand next to their matching letter.

Capital and Lowercase Collage
Have children find capital and lowercase letters in a magazine. Help them cut the letters out and paste them on a piece of construction paper. Create a page per letter.

Match Makers

Match Capital & Lowercase Letters

Matching is an important cognitive skill for Pre-K children. They love to match capital and lowercase letters. This skill helps them understand that there is one alphabet, even though there are two cases. Then, when they begin to attach sounds to letters, they will associate the same sounds with matching capital and lowercase letters.

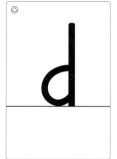 

Look What We're Learning

Alphabet Knowledge
- Match all capital and lowercase letters

Social-Emotional
- Cooperate with other children
- Take turns

Sensory Motor
- Move an object in one hand to position it for use

Vocabulary

match

Match Makers

Materials/Setup:
Materials/Setup:
- Sound Around Box™:
  - Magnetic Pieces for Capitals
- A-B-C Touch & Flip® Cards

Grouping:
Small group; Whole class

English Language Learners:
Have children use complete sentences when they name capital and lowercase letters. "This is capital D. This is lowercase d."

Objective
Children recognize and match capital and lowercase letters.

Activity
Let's find a lowercase letter that matches my capital.

1. Make capital **D** with Magnetic Pieces on the side of the Sound Around Box.

2. Place two A-B-C Touch & Flip Cards in the Sound Around Box. Use lowercase **d** and another lowercase letter.

3. **Who can reach in the box and help us find lowercase d?**

4. Have a child reach in the box and hold up both cards.

5. Ask the class to choose the lowercase letter that matches capital **D**.

6. Repeat with other letters.

✓ Check for Understanding
Observe children making matches. Do they choose the correct match?

Support: Introduce only two to three letters at a time. When children match and name **C c / O o** easily, add one more. Keep the ones that children already know **C c / O o / S s**. Continue with **U u, V v, W w, X x, Y y**.

More to Learn

Circle a Letter
To add interest, write two lowercase **d**s and two other letters on the Sound Around Box. Allow students to come forward and circle the two lowercase **d**s.

Challenging Match
For more of a challenge, add more lowercase and capital letters. Or, leave out the matching letter and have children say, "There is not a match this time."

CONCEPTS ABOUT PRINT
All About Books

To learn to read, children must learn how books work, and develop what educators call Concepts About Print. These concepts include: 1) parts of a book—front, back, spine, title, author, and illustrator; 2) how to hold a book right-side up; 3) how to turn pages from front to back; and 4) how to read from top to bottom and left to right. Though most of us demonstrate these concepts regularly as we read to our children, we need to teach them explicitly.

Children's knowledge of these concepts when they enter kindergarten is a major factor in future reading success (Nichols, Rupley, Rickleman, & Algozzine, 2004). Children should know that both print and pictures have meaning, but that the print or words on the page is what is being read. It is important that children understand that print is all around them. Print in our environment helps us understand where to go and what to do (signs, directions for assembling a toy).

The activities in this domain help children learn to:

- **Distinguish Print from Pictures**
- **Recognize Book Parts**
- **Follow Text Top to Bottom, Left to Right**
- **Distinguish Letters, Words, and Sentences**
- **Recognize Names**
- **Recognize Signs**

Below is the significant research for this domain. For additional Concepts About Print resources, see the reference section at the end of this teacher's guide.

Adams, M.J. 1990. *Beginning to read: Thinking and Learning about Print.* Cambridge, MA: MIT Press.

Beauchat, K.A., K.L. Blamey, and S. Walpole. 2009. "Building Preschool Children's Language and Literacy One Storybook at a Time." *The Reading Teacher* 63(1): 26-39.

Nichols, W., W. Rupley, R. Rickelman, and B. Algozzine. 2004. "Examining Phonemic Awareness and Concepts of Print Patterns of Kindergarten Students." *Reading Research and Instruction* 43(3):56-82.

My Book

My Book is a child's personal storybook. Your children are the authors and illustrators. Because the story is personalized, children are motivated to read the book many times. Through these repeated readings, children learn what educators call "Concepts About Print." Understanding concepts about print is a beginning step in reading. Children learn how printed language works and how books are organized. The inside pages of My Book have black and white pictures that invite drawing and coloring. You introduce the page(s) with a brief description. The children tell you how to personalize each page. You write the words the children say.

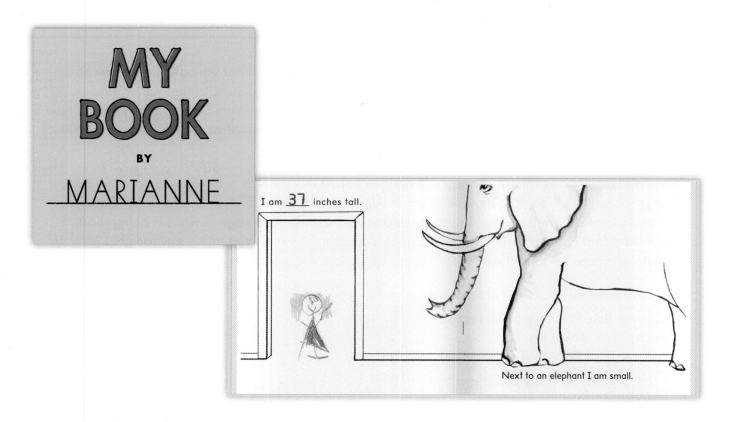

You'll like it because . . .

My Book can be used one-on-one, in small groups, or in a whole class setting. It captures children's thoughts through personal drawings, colorings, and words. Children learn how to hold a book right-side up, identify book parts inside and out, and tell what's on the cover. They learn the way people read and look at pages to make sense of the pictures and words. When My Book is complete, they will want to share their books with everyone—teachers, friends, and family. What better way for children to learn about books than to read an engaging, creative book about themselves?

Where you'll see it

Concepts About Print	Writing
Comprehension	

Discovery Teaching in Your Day

Concepts About Print

Old Favorites

You're already teaching concepts about print. You do this informally every time you read aloud, stand books up for display, or put books away. Children watch as you put books on the shelf with the spines out and set up a book display. They notice how as you read to them and learn from you by exposure.

You're already teaching explicitly too. You teach them book words as you read to them. "I'm going to read _____. That's the title, the name of the book" You use big books to show how reading goes. You move your finger to demonstrate reading from top to bottom, and across lines from left to right. You do return sweeps to show the next line starts at the left.

Have You Tried These?

Pass and Discover: Pass a basket of picture books. Watch children discover the different choices. Read the title to each child. Ask why she chose it and what she can tell from the illustrations.

Book Helpers: Let children help you sort, display, and shelve books (animal, ABC, 123, etc.). When children work together, they learn from each other.

Child's Choice: Once a week, let a child choose the book to read. Talk to the child about the book, letting him be a book critic and give a book review.

More than Story Books: Show children comic books, cookbooks, dictionaries, map books, art books. Also show them the latest book technology.

Mix in Some Get Set for School® Activities

My Book: *My Book* is an ideal book for explicitly teaching book parts. Children love to hear you tell everything about *My Book* because you're talking about a book they wrote.

Mat Man®: The Mat Man book series also engages children because he's a favorite character who explores concepts that are fun and familiar. They know Mat Man from the stories and from their hands-on play: they build Mat Man, sing about Mat Man along with the CDs, and learn to draw people with him.

Pictures & Words

Distinguish Print from Pictures

Children see print and pictures all around their homes, school, and community. Before they can read, they recognize signs, such as traffic and fast food signs. Children need to understand that pictures and print have meaning. Pictures show people, animals, places, or things. Print represents spoken words on paper. Children need to recognize that pictures are different from print.

pizza

carrots

blueberries

Food has colors: red, orange, and blue.

© 2011 Get Set for School

Look What We're Learning

Concepts About Print
- Distinguish print from pictures
- Understand that print can be read and has meaning

Vocabulary

picture
word

Pictures & Words

Materials/Setup:
• *My Book*

Grouping:
Small group; Whole class

English Language Learners:
Put Picture Tiles in the Sound Around Box™. Have the student pull a tile from the box. **This is a picture. It is a picture of a dog.** Have child place the tile on the box. **I'm going to write the word dog for you.** Write "dog" next to the tile. Once you have two to three picture tiles and words on the box, ask children to point to a picture and then to a word.

Objective
Children recognize the difference between print and pictures and that both have meaning.

Activity
Pictures are different from printed words. We look at pictures and we read words.

1. **What is the name of your book? Yes, you're right. The title is *My Book.***

2. **In *My Book*, I found a picture of a playground.** Show picture.

3. **I bet you can find a picture, too.** Have children look through *My Book* to find a different picture.

4. When it's time to share, have children say, **In *My Book*, I found a picture of a carrot.**

5. Repeat activity with words. **In *My Book*, I found a word.** Point to the word. **Now you find a word. Show me your word. Your word says, food.**

✓ Check for Understanding

Observe children as they show pictures and words. Can they distinguish between pictures and print?

Support: Put several picture tiles and their matching words in the Sound Around Box. Have students pull an item from the box and identify it as a picture or a word.

More to Learn

Picture Search
Help each child cut a picture from a magazine and paste it on a plain sheet of paper. Label each picture with the word. Display the pictures.

Words Tell a Story
For more of a challenge, show the children a scenic picture from a book or a magazine. For each picture, have the children tell you a short story with two or three sentences. Write the story on the board so they can see that the words represent what they say.

Book Parts

Recognize Book Parts

Children are fascinated by books. They enjoy being read to and imitating reading in play. When they can identify parts of a book and use picture clues, they learn to hold a book right-side up. Then they can see the print correctly and learn to identify the different elements: title, name of the author and/or illustrator. Learning that print carries meaning is an essential pre-reading skill.

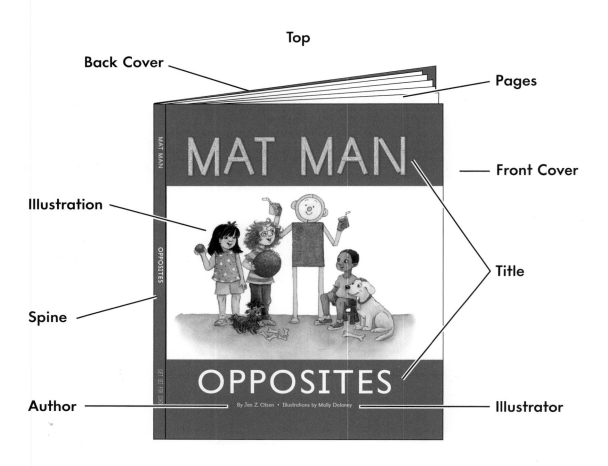

Look What We're Learning

Concepts About Print

- Hold book right-side up
- Open book at title page
- Point to front cover, back cover, pages, and spine
- Point to the title, author, and illustrator of a book
- Say what titles, authors, and illustrators do

Vocabulary

front cover	outside
back cover	top
spine	bottom
title	title page
author	
illustrator	

Book Parts

Materials/Setup:
- *Mat Man Opposites*
- Children's books, one per child

Grouping:
One-on-one; Small group; or Whole class

English Language Learners:
Help children understand front and back, by showing the front/back of different items in the classroom, e.g., the front/back of their bodies, a chair, a desk. Have children repeat words.

Objective
Children hold a book right-side up. They identify the front and back covers, spine, top and bottom, and title page. They recognize the title, author and/or illustrator on the front cover, and title page.

Activity
Let's learn about books. Books have different parts.

1. Show *Mat Man Opposites* and point to the front and back covers and spine.

2. Have children point to the front and back covers and spine of their books.

3. Have children point to the top and bottom of their books.

4. Read the author's name. **The author writes the words.** Read the illustrator's name. **The illustrator draws the pictures. Their names are on the cover and title page.**

5. Have children point to the author's and/or illustrator's names on the front cover and title page of their books.

✓ Check for Understanding

Observe children holding their books. Can they identify the different book parts?

Support: Compare a person and a book:

A person has a front.	A book has a front.
A person has a name.	A book has a name, the title.
A person has a spine.	A book has a spine.
A person has a back.	A book has a back.
A person can walk.	Can a book walk? No, but a book can take you on a trip to another place.

More to Learn

Book Show and Tell
Have children select their favorite books. Ask them to show the different parts of their books. Have them point out the author and illustrator's names on the front cover and title page and say what each one does.

Predict It
For a challenge, show the front cover and title page of a book. Read the title and have children say what they think will happen in the book. Read and talk about the book. Ask children what they would tell the author and/or illustrator about the book.

Which Way Do We Go?

Follow Text Left to Right

Children love to mimic how others read. They move their fingers over the pages and turn the pages as if they are actually reading. Children must learn to read from top to bottom and left to right to develop literacy.

Look What We're Learning

Concepts About Print
- Imitate reading behaviors when handling books
- Turn pages from front to back, one at a time
- Follow print from top to bottom, left to right on a page
- Point to print moving left to right; sweep to next line, starting at left

Comprehension
- Enjoy books and reading activities

Vocabulary

pages   left
front   right
back   words
top
bottom

Which Way Do We Go?

Materials/Setup:
- *My Book,* one per child

Grouping:
Small group; Whole class

English Language Learners:
Place a hula hoop on the floor. Let children take a turn standing inside the hula hoop and have them say "inside." Repeat for outside. Have them point to the top of their head and say "top." Repeat for bottom and have them point to their feet.

Objective
Children learn how to turn pages and read from top to bottom and left to right.

Activity
Let's open a book and read what's inside.

1. Review the outside parts of *My Book.*

2. **Let's look inside. Pages are inside. Pages have pictures and words.**

3. **Watch my finger as I read the words. I start at the top. I read words from left to right.**

4. Have children pretend to read in their copies of *My Book* from top to bottom, left to right and return sweep.

5. Turn the page and continue reading. Have children turn the page with you.

✓ Check for Understanding

Have children choose their favorite books. Observe them as they turn the pages in the book. Do they "read" from top to bottom, left to right, and return sweep?

Support: Have children complete some pages in *My Book.* Point to the beginning of a sentence and drag your finger to the right. Have them say, "I start on the left and move to the right. That's how I read."

More to Learn

All Kinds of Pages
Demonstrate reading in a variety of page layouts. The text may be above or below the picture.

Follow the Words
Take a pile of four to six books, have children open them and find the first word to read in each book. Have them pretend to read, running their fingers over the words.

Letters & Words for Sentences

Distinguish Letters, Words & Sentences

Children recognize and name single letters. They learn that words are made with letters and that sentences are made with words. Initially, they will not always understand the distinction but must learn to do so to understand how to read.

Look What We're Learning

Concepts About Print
• Distinguish between a written sentence, word, and letter

Vocabulary

letter
word
sentence
scroll

Letters & Words for Sentences

Materials/Setup:
- Small basket
- Marker
- Scroll rolls

Grouping:
Small group; Whole class

English Language Learners:
Write a four-letter word on an index card. Show children the word, **Word**. Have them repeat. Cut the word into four separate letters. Show children a letter, **Letter**. Have them repeat. Reassemble the word. Repeat activity for a sentence.

Objective
Children recognize letters, words, and sentences by observing their different characteristics.

Activity
A scroll is a rolled up piece of paper. See my little scrolls? Let's unroll them and see what's inside.

1. Prepare scrolls: one letter, one word, one sentence. Roll and place scrolls in the basket.

2. Have a child choose a scroll and unroll it.

3. As the child unrolls his scroll, ask, **Is it a letter? . . . or a word? . . . or a sentence?** If it's a letter, say, **Look, it's a letter. It's all alone.** For a word: **Look, it's a letter. Oh wait! It's a word.** For a sentence: **Look, it's a letter. No, it's a word. Wait, it's a sentence!**

4. Place scrolls on the floor or hang them up to be compared.

✓ Check for Understanding
Observe children as they open additional scrolls and sort them into letters, words, and sentences. Do they identify each correctly?

Support: Use A-B-C Touch & Flip® Cards and Word Time™ Word Cards. Mix the cards together. Have children sort Letter Cards in one pile and Word Cards in another pile.

More to Learn

Words and Letters in Our Room
Have children point to words around the classroom or school. Write the words for the group to see. Say the letters of each word together. Say the word in a sentence.

Sentences about Me
Have children say action words for things they like to do, e.g., play, run, sing. Guide them to say sentences, such as, "I play soccer." Draw pictures and write the sentences on their papers. Have them point to a letter, word, and sentence.

I Know My Name & Your Name, Too

Recognize Names

Children love to hear and see their names and play different games with them. Because children's names are very important to them, they quickly learn to identify their own names. They also like to identify their friends' names. When they do this, they reinforce alphabet knowledge and begin to attach sounds to letters.

Look What We're Learning

Concepts About Print
- Recognize own name in print
- Recognize the names of friends and family in print

Vocabulary

name
capital letters
first

I Know My Name & Your Name, Too

Objective
Children recognize their own names and their friends' names.

Activity
Let's learn the names of our classmates as we sing a song.

1. Sing "I'm Happy to See You" using each child's name.

2. The child whose name is being sung should stand. As you sing, hold up the Name Card with the child's name on it.

3. After singing, read the child's name. **Ava, A-V-A, Ava.** Have class repeat after you.

4. Gather all of the Name Cards. Distribute them randomly. **Look at the name on the card. Go find that friend.**

✓ Check for Understanding

Add a picture of the child to the back of his/her Name Card. Hold up the Name Card. **Whose name is this? It begins with the letter A.** Do children recognize whose name it is? Flip over the card to reveal the answer.

Support: Help children finger trace the beginning letter of their names using the tactile letters from A-B-C Touch & Flip® Cards.

More to Learn

Sticky Names
Post the Line It Up™ Letter Cards around the room. Give each child a sticky note with his/her name written on it. Say a beginning letter and ask all children with a name that begins with that letter to come up and put their sticky note on the posted letter.

Famous Faces
Choose pictures of famous people and write their names for children. Tell something about each person. Does anyone in the class share a first or last name or another fact with a famous person?

I Can Read Signs!

Recognize Signs

Children see signs all around. Familiar elements help them recognize sign words by sight. Children learn to recognize bathroom, safety, directional, and many other functional signs.

Look What We're Learning

Concepts About Print
- Recognize important signs in our world

Comprehension
- Listen to gain and share information
- Enjoy books and reading activities

Math
- Sort objects by shape

Vocabulary

sign

Materials/Setup:
• Camera

Grouping:
Small group; Whole class

English Language Learners:
Show a stop sign. **Stop signs are red. Let's practice how to stop.** Have children walk around the room until you hold up the stop sign and say, **Stop**.

Objective
Children recognize important signs in our world.

Activity
There are many signs in our world. Let's look at some of them.

1. Read a book about signs and invite children to point out signs in the book.

2. **Let's go on a walk. We will take pictures of the signs we see.** Take a walk and encourage children to point out any signs they find.

3. Print the photos.

4. Invite children to sort the signs by shape. Display in the classroom.

To have children make their own sign, see "Sign Makers" on pages 162–163.

✓ Check for Understanding

Show children other signs around the school. Do they understand the meaning of the signs?

Support: Put red octagons on the floor. Have children walk until they reach a red octagon. As they walk, have them say, "Walk, walk, walk." When they reach the red octagon, have them stop and shout, "Stop!"

More to Learn

Push and Pull
Add interest by having children check all the doors in the classroom to see if they open with a pull or push. Label the doors accordingly.

Cut and Color
Help children cut out the signs (printed from A Click Away). Trace crayon stroke letters. Have children color the signs. Place signs at appropriate places around the classroom or school.

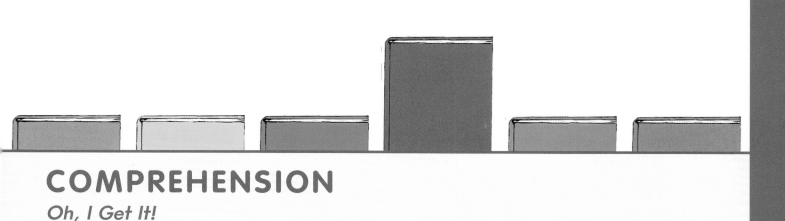

COMPREHENSION
Oh, I Get It!

Comprehension is a fundamental building block of literacy development. But what does it mean for Pre-K children? Young children begin to make sense of things very early and try to make meaning from what they hear, see, and experience. They make meaning from stories that are read to them and through self-directed play and dramatic play experiences. Vocabulary is also essential for comprehension. As children gain experiences, they build the vocabulary for understanding what they hear. Your classroom activities will contribute to vocabulary development.

Educators refer to making sense of information that we experience as comprehension. As with learning to read, children need to learn how to understand what they experience through their senses.

Children learn the importance of comprehension and use their memories and pictures to make sense of what happens in a story. Comprehension skills in Pre-K provide a solid foundation for children to grow and become thoughtful listeners, speakers, readers, and writers.

The activities in this domain help children to:
- **Make Predictions**
- **Recognize Beginning, Middle, and End**
- **Find Main Character**
- **Name the Place**
- **Describe Problem and Solution**
- **Identify Emotions in a Story**
- **Distinguish Real from Make-Believe**
- **Make Personal Connections**
- **Make Connections Between Stories**
- **Retell a Story**
- **Find Facts**
- **Sort Information**

Below is the significant research for this domain. For additional Comprehension resources, see the reference section at the end of this teacher's guide.

Cunningham, A. E., and K.E. Stanovich. 1997. "Early Reading Acquisition and Its Relation to Reading Experience and Ability 10 Years Later." *Developmental Psychology* 33(6):934-945.

Morrow, L. 2005. *Literacy development in the early years: Helping children read and write (5th ed.).* Boston: Allyn & Bacon.

Spear-Swerling, L. 2006. "Children's Reading Comprehension and Oral Reading Fluency in Easy Text." *Reading & Writing: An Interdisciplinary Journal* 19:199-220.

Line It Up™

Line It Up Story Cards engage children with activities that develop critical early literacy skills. There are five stories in all—two nonfiction and three fiction: "Growing Pumpkins" (nonfiction), "How a Butterfly Grows" (nonfiction), "Isabel's Birthday" (fiction), "Ready for Robins" (fiction), "Little Miss Muffet" (fiction).

The set includes:
- 15 Story Cards (3 per story)
  - Story illustrations (front)
  - Ideas for exploring literacy, math, and science (back)
- Activity instruction pamphlets (5, one for each story)
  - Teach important vocabulary, check for comprehension, and provide instructions
  - Recommend books connected to the story
- Line It Up Bar
  - Unique display bar that holds cards in place while allowing children to place cards in, out, and around the bar

You'll like them because . . .

Line It Up Story Cards introduce preschoolers to several literacy basics. After hearing colorful fiction and nonfiction stories, children answer questions, sequence cards, and retell the story. The cards are interactive and invite children to handle them, to point out a picture, to make a personal connection, or to retell the story. Children practice listening, using their memories, and communicating about make-believe stories, nursery rhymes, and informational text. They can learn about how a butterfly or a pumpkin grows, make personal connections to Isabel's birthday, learn about robins, and find out why Little Miss Muffet was frightened away. Use activities in this teacher's guide, the activity pamphlets, the back of the Story Cards, or create your own exercises to make the most of the Line It Up Story Cards.

Where you'll see them

Comprehension   Writing

Discovery Teaching in Your Day

Comprehension

Old Favorites

Regular Read Aloud: Reading aloud is one of the most powerful literacy building practices. It has the most impact when the reader expands on the book while reading. The comprehension skills children learn as they listen will help them when they begin to read books themselves.

Preview and Predict: Show the front cover. Read the title, author, and illustrator's names. Ask children what they think the story will be about. Show each illustration in the book. Ask children for additional or revised predictions. Discuss predictions after reading. Were they correct? What really happened?

Whys and What Ifs: Guide children to think further about characters' thoughts, feelings, and actions. **Why did the puppy stop playing? What would happen if the lion were kind to the mouse?**

After You're Done: Review any new words from the text. Ask children questions and talk about their favorite parts of the book. Encourage them to relate the text to their own lives. Children will also enjoy retelling the stories in their own words.

Have You Tried These?

Go for Drama: Act out stories. Add props from texts to the dramatic play center. Puppets, stuffed animals, and a felt board are all fun to use.

Hit Replay: Read the same books multiple times. Change your emphasis each time, for example, vocabulary, characters, illustrations.

Give a Hook: Tell a bit of the story, but don't give it all away.

My Favorite Part: Have children share their favorite parts. Have each child draw part of the story and dictate a description. Compile these into a class book.

Mix in Some Get Set for School® Activities

Grow Your Library: Add books that you've read to the classroom library. Include books that the class has written together and copies of *My Book*. Children will re-read them many times.

Line It Up™: These Story Cards offer a variety of interesting learning opportunities. You'll notice different illustration styles, different types of stories (fiction, nonfiction, nursery rhyme), and extension activities. There will be many opportunities for you to make connections between these stories and your regular classroom reading. These cards can be a useful reference point as you explain other books and stories.

What Will Happen?

Make Predictions

When children can predict, they can better link prior knowledge, observation, thinking, and active listening. Children use illustrations and prior knowledge to make predictions. They ask questions, make guesses, and draw conclusions. This approach to reading engages children in the story and boosts comprehension.

Look What We're Learning

Comprehension
- Make a prediction about a book by looking at pictures and illustrations
- Use prior knowledge to make predictions about a story
- Listen to learn what happened in a story
- Listen to converse with an adult or peer

Vocabulary

predict
prediction
title

What Will Happen?

Materials/Setup:
• Children's book

Grouping:
Small group; Whole class

English Language Learners:
Before you do the activity, preview the objects in the book's illustrations. Have children repeat the names of the objects. When you do the activity, children will be more familiar with the vocabulary and story.

Objective
Children predict what will happen in a story.

Activity
I am going to read a book. Before I read, let's predict what will happen. Predict means to tell what will happen before we really know.

1. Show children the front cover. **What do you see in the picture? What do you predict will happen in this story?** Listen, and ask why children made their predictions. Write down the predictions if you like.

2. Read the title. **Now that you know the title, what do you predict will happen? Did your prediction change?**

3. Begin reading aloud. Stop once or twice to get any new or updated predictions.

4. Review the children's predictions after reading. Compare them with what really happened. **What did we predict, or say would happen? What really happened?**

✓ Check for Understanding

Notice how and why the children make their predictions. Do their predictions make sense? Do their predictions change based on additional information?

Support: Show Line It Up™ Story Card 1 from "Isabel's Birthday." Have children predict what will happen. Read the story.

More to Learn

Pumpkin Life
Use "Growing Pumpkins" Story Cards from Line It Up. Show each picture and ask for predictions. Have children predict what is growing. Read the title and story after predictions have been made.

It's in the Name
For a challenge, have children predict what will happen after only hearing the title of the story. Have them draw pictures showing their predictions and talk about them. Then read the story. For more fun, have children dictate a new story with that title.

Beginning, Middle & End

Recognize Beginning, Middle & End

When children can identify the sequence of beginning, middle, and end, they can better comprehend the story and make sense of what they have heard or read. This understanding enables them to organize their memories and retell stories.

Look What We're Learning

Comprehension

- Identify the beginning, middle, and end of a story
- Order the events of a story correctly using pictures
- Listen to gain and share information
- Listen to learn what happened in a story

- Retell story or event with pictures
- Re-enact a story or event

Vocabulary

beginning

middle

end

first

next

last

Beginning, Middle & End

Materials/Setup:

- Line It Up™:
  - Magnetic Bar
  - "Ready for Robins" Story Cards

Grouping:
Small group; Whole class

English Language Learners:
Help children understand beginning, middle, and end. Have three children line up. Point out who is at the beginning, middle, and end. You can also line up other classroom items and point out the beginning, middle, and end of each line.

Objective
Children identify the beginning, middle, and end of a story.

Activity
Try to remember what happens in the beginning, middle, and end of our story.

1. Read "Ready for Robins."

2. Have children pretend to be young robins. **I will be your robin parent. Here is our nice warm nest. Pretend you are my small blue eggs. Roll into a small egg. You can't see. You don't have feathers. You are very hungry. Now, break out of your shell. Here are some yummy worms. Open wide! You get stronger. You can see and grow feathers. Now, try your wings out and fly. Beautiful!**

3. Place Story Cards in the Line It Up Bar out of order. Re-read words for the first card. **Show me what happens first. Please put it up.**

4. Re-read the words for the second card. **Show me the picture of what happens next. Please put it next to the first card.**

5. Re-read the words for the third card. **Show me the picture of what happens last. Please put it next to the second card.**

6. **Now we know the beginning, middle, and end of the story.**

✓ Check for Understanding

Observe as children retell the story. Can they identify the beginning, middle and end? Can they sequence the story?

Support: Show a real banana. **I am going to share this banana. What should I do first?** (Peel.) **And next?** (Slice, share, and eat.) **And next?** (Throw away the peel.)

More to Learn

Draw & Act It Out
Read a book to your children. As a class, help children draw three pictures that represent the beginning, middle, and end. Have three groups of 3–4 children act out the beginning, middle, or end of the book. Let the groups present their parts in sequence. Hold up the appropriate drawing while acting.

"Ballet Dancing Truck Driver"
Play "Ballet Dancing Truck Driver," track 29 on the *Sing, Sound & Count With Me* CD. Have children try to remember the jobs in order. Take pictures of the children wearing a hat to go with a job in the song. Have fun ordering the pictures while playing the song.

Who Could It Be?

Find the Main Character

We want children to understand what they read (and what is read to them). Teaching story elements directs their focus to the key parts of the story. The most basic story element is the main character. Children need to identify about whom the story is written.

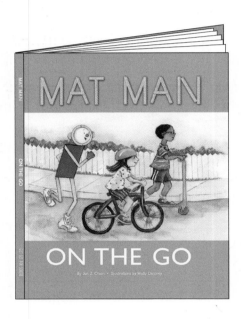

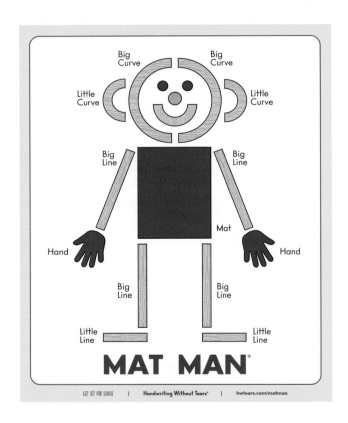

Look What We're Learning

Comprehension
- Identify the main character in a story
- Listen to learn what happened in a story
- Retell story or event with pictures
- Demonstrate interest in read aloud time

Social-Emotional
- Take turns
- Cooperate with other children

Sensory Motor
- Naturally move and place body to perform tasks

Vocabulary

main character

Materials/Setup:

- *Mat Man On the Go*
- Wood Pieces
  - 4 Big Lines
  - 2 Little Lines
  - 2 Big Curves
  - 3 Little Curves
- Mat
- Cutout hands
- Three or four bottle caps
- *Get Set for School Sing Along* CD, track 8, "Mat Man" (optional)

Grouping:
Whole class

English Language Learners:
Read *Mat Man Hats*. As you look at each picture, point out Mat Man each time he appears. **The main character is usually in a lot of pictures. Who do you see? Mat Man. Who do you see on this page? Mat Man!**

Objective
Children identify the main character in a story.

Activity
Who is the most important person in the story? Listen to find out.

1. Read *Mat Man On the Go* to the class.

2. **Who was the most important person in the story?** (Mat Man®.)

3. **I see some other people in the book. How do you know Mat Man is the most important one?** Children may say that he is on every page.

4. **We call Mat Man the main character because he is the most important person in the story. Let's build Mat Man together.**

5. Pass out Wood Pieces, Mat, hands, and bottle caps to build Mat Man. Have children come forward and place their pieces in turn. You can sing "Mat Man" to prompt the building.

✓ Check for Understanding

Read another book to the class. Can children identify the main character?

Support: Show children two series of books, for example, *Mat Man* and *Clifford the Big Red Dog*. Hold up the books and have children name the main character in the book. Put the books into piles according to the main character.

More to Learn

More Adventures Ahead
Select a story with a single main character. Read the story and show children the pictures in the book. Ask children to identify the main character. Discuss their choice. Ask what other adventure this character could have.

Who's the Main One?
Add a challenge by reading a story with several characters. Have children share their ideas about the main character. Direct them to the illustrations, and talk about who does most of the actions.

What Can You See?

Name the Place
The setting is a key element of stories. Being able to recognize setting helps children understand what happens in a story and why. It also increases their awareness of their own surroundings.

Look What We're Learning

Comprehension
- Say where a story takes place
- Listen for enjoyment
- Listen to gain and share information
- Listen to converse with an adult or peer

Social-Emotional
- Take turns
- Cooperate with other children

Sensory Motor
- Naturally move and place body to perform tasks

Vocabulary

setting

What Can You See?

Materials/Setup:

- Children's book with vivid setting
- Toilet paper tubes, two per child
- 2-Feet pieces of string or yarn
- Stapler

Grouping:
Small group

English Language Learners:

Read a story with a familiar setting. Show children that there are clues in the illustrations. Point out and name things in the illustrations that show where the story is happening.

Objective
Children identify the setting of a story.

Activity
We're going to look at where a story happens.

1. Help children make play binoculars by holding their tubes side by side as you staple them together. Staple each end of the string to the top outside edges of the binoculars. This step can be done anytime prior to reading the story.

2. **We made binoculars. Binoculars help people look carefully at things in a place. Real ones make things look bigger too.**

3. **Let's try our binoculars. Look around the room. What do you see?** Have volunteers tell what they see.

4. **While I read the story, look carefully through your binoculars at the pictures. Think about the places that are in the pictures.** Read the story aloud.

5. **Okay, now let your binoculars hang around your neck. What did you see in the pictures? Where did the story happen? How do you know?**

6. **The place where a story happens is called the setting. The setting can also tell when a story happens. You might know the setting is in the winter because children are building a snowman.**

✓ Check for Understanding

Read another book to the class. Can children tell where (and when) the story happened?

Support: Show "Isabel's Birthday" Story Cards. Say, **I see an oven. I see a table. Where could this be? Is the oven in the bedroom? The park? The bathroom?**

More to Learn

Set the Stage
Discuss acting out a favorite story. Talk about how people presenting a play set up props and scenery to show where the story is happening. **What things could we put on the stage to show the setting?** Gather props, make some simple scenery, and have children act out the story.

Where Could It Be?
Add a challenge by having children imagine that a story is happening in a different season or in a different place.

What Should I Do?

Describe Problem & Solution

Children understand that when they have a problem, they want to work it out. When they find a solution, they feel better. Many stories contain some type of problem for the characters to solve. Children learn that just as they feel better when their problems are solved, stories feel complete when the character's problem is solved.

Look What We're Learning

Comprehension

- Describe the problem and solution of a story
- Listen to stories, plays, and poems and talk about their meaning
- Explain how a story connects to personal experience

Social-Emotional

- Name emotions displayed by others

Vocabulary

problem

solution

What Should I Do?

Materials/Setup:
- Line It Up™:
  – Magnetic Bar
  – "Little Miss Muffet" Story Cards
- Book of nursery rhymes

Grouping:
Small group; Whole class

English Language Learners:
Draw a spider and then invite all the children to draw a spider. Repeat the word **spider** several times.

Objective
Children describe the problem and solution of a story.

Activity
Let's talk about problems and solutions.

1. **Have you ever lost a favorite toy? Have you ever broken something? These could be problems. How could we solve these problems?** Invite children to share examples.

2. **A story can have a problem and a solution. Listen to this story about Little Miss Muffet.** Read the Story Cards one at a time. Place them in the Line It Up Bar.

3. **What was Miss Muffet's problem?**

4. **How did she fix it?**

5. **What would you do if a spider came and sat beside you?** Have children share their creative solutions to Miss Muffet's problem.

✓ Check for Understanding

Read another nursery rhyme with a problem and solution. Are children able to identify the problem and solution?

Support: Present different problem situations. **If <u>it snows</u>, then what should you do?** Have props available.

If you are going outside and it's raining, then what should you do? (You should use an umbrella.)

If there is trash on the floor, then what should you do? (You should put it in the trash can.)

If you are thirsty, then what should you do? (You should drink water.)

More to Learn

What Could They Do?
Read a story that contains a problem. Pause after the problem is described. Have children identify the problem. Then predict different ways that the characters can solve the problem.

Solution Twist
Read a story or poem with a problem that could be solved in many different ways. What if the characters had solved the problem differently? Draw a picture to show a different solution. Have children tell you what to draw and invite them to add details and color the drawing.

Feelings Are Important

Identify Emotions in a Story

Children have feelings about what happens to them. Characters in stories have feelings too. Something that happens in a story may make a character happy, sad, scared, or mad. Illustrations help children understand what's happening and how the characters are feeling. How the characters feel shows the tone of the story. The tone of the story changes as the characters react to what happens.

sad   happy   scared   mad

Look What We're Learning

Comprehension
- Identify and name emotions in story
- Explain how a story connects to personal experience

Social-Emotional
- Name emotions displayed by others
- Show empathy to others

Vocabulary

feelings

sad

happy

scared

mad

Feelings Are Important

Materials/Setup:

- Craft sticks
- Tape or glue
- Line It Up™ Story Cards, "Little Miss Muffet"
- Feeling Faces cutouts

Grouping:
Small group; Whole class

English Language Learners:
Preview vocabulary: **happy**, **sad**, **scared**, and **mad** with Feeling Faces cutouts. Take photographs of your children practicing faces that show these emotions and have them name the emotions they see in the photos.

Objective
Children detect the feelings of characters in a story.

Activity
We can have many different feelings—happy, sad, scared, mad, or others. Let's listen and think about how the characters in our story feel.

1. Make Feeling Faces by having children fold them and glue each one to a stick. Each child should make a set of four. You can do this step anytime prior to reading the story.

2. Read "Little Miss Muffet." Talk about the first card. **What is happening?** (She is eating.) **How do you feel when you're eating? How does Miss Muffet feel?** (She is happy.) **Children, hold up the happy face.**

3. Talk about the next card. **What is happening?** (A spider came.) **How does Miss Muffet feel?** (She is scared.) **How do you feel when you see a spider? Children, hold up the scared face.**

4. Talk about the last card. **What is happening?** (She is running away.) **How would she feel then?** Listen to the variety of emotions children share.

✓ Check for Understanding

Listen to children's responses and observe as they display their cutouts. Do children name the expected feeling? Do they hold up the correct Feeling Face?

Support: Start with only two Feeling Faces: happy and sad.

More to Learn

How Would You Feel?
Describe scenarios and ask children to hold up the Feeling Face that shows how they would feel. For example, **You dropped your ice cream on the ground. Your soccer team won the game!**

Finding Feelings
Have partners share a book and look for faces. Have them share with each other about what feeling is shown.

Is It Real?

Distinguish Real from Make-Believe

When they read some books, children will encounter things that are real. In other books, they will come across things that are imaginary. It is important to identify features that indicate whether a book is real or make-believe. This skill is a foundation for children to understand the difference between nonfiction and fiction.

Look What We're Learning

Comprehension
- Identify parts of stories that are real and not real
- Listen to gain and share information

Vocabulary

real

make-believe

Materials/Setup:

- An informational picture book (with photographs) about pigs
- *The Three Little Pigs*

Grouping:

Small group; Whole class

English Language Learners:

Ask children how to say real and make-believe in their home languages. Show pictures of real and make-believe animals from children's books. Have children say which are real and which are make-believe using English words and words in their home languages.

Objective

Children differentiate between real and make-believe.

Activity

Let's look at two books. Can you tell which is about real things and which is about make-believe things?

1. **In books there are things that are real and there are things that are not real. Things that are not real are called make-believe.**

2. Show pictures from the informational book. Read some of the facts. **Do these pictures look real or make-believe? Tell me some real information you heard about pigs from the book.**

3. Read and show pictures from the beginning of *The Three Little Pigs*. **Do real pigs wear clothes? Can real pigs talk? This story is make-believe.**

4. Show other pictures from *The Three Little Pigs*. Ask children to point out things that real pigs could not do.

5. Repeat this activity frequently with other make-believe animal stories and informational books about the same kinds of animals.

✓ Check for Understanding

Read parts of a fairy tale. Are children able to identify the difference between real and make-believe?

Support: Continue this real versus make-believe activity with other animal stories, such as "The Little Red Hen." Ask, **Do hens cook in kitchens?**

More to Learn

Tell Your Own Tale

Have small groups of children choose an animal. Have the groups dictate real information or a make-believe story about that animal. Write their stories on chart paper to re-read and share with the whole class.

Book Sort

Select children's books—both informational and make-believe—from the library. Have children look at and sort the books into real and make-believe piles.

Just Like Me

Make Personal Connections

The connection of personal experiences with stories adds meaning and enjoyment to reading. How many times have you really liked a book because you could identify with a character? Children also love to make these connections. The skill helps them understand stories and encourages emotional ties that fuel a love of reading.

Look What We're Learning

Comprehension
- Explain how a story connects to personal experience
- Listen to converse with an adult or peer
- Enjoy books and reading activities

Oral Language
- Share opinions and ideas in conversation and discussion

Social-Emotional
- Name feelings he or she is experiencing
- Name emotions displayed by others

Vocabulary

feelings

Materials/Setup:
- Line It Up™:
  - Magnetic Bar
  - "Isabel's Birthday" Story Cards
- *Sing, Sound & Count With Me* CD, track 9, "Counting Candles"

Grouping:
Small group; Whole class

English Language Learners:
Ask children how they celebrate birthdays in their families. Is there special food or a special song? Allow children to share with their classmates.

Objective
Children make personal connections with stories.

Activity
Have you ever done something just like what happened in a story? That helps us understand the story. Let's read a story like that.

1. Read "Isabel's Birthday." After you read each card, hand it to a child to place on the bar.

2. **If you have ever had a birthday, please stand up. Wow! Look! Everyone in our class has had a birthday. Okay, let's sit back down.**

3. **How do you feel on your birthday?** (Happy.) (Excited.) **How do you think Isabel feels?** (Happy.) (Excited.) **We know how Isabel might feel because we have also had birthdays.**

4. **What else could happen on Isabel's birthday? How do you know?**

5. Play "Counting Candles." **Let's sing this song about a birthday and put in Isabel's name.**

✓ Check for Understanding

Listen to children's responses to your questions about what else could happen on Isabel's birthday and how they know. Are they able to make personal connections with the story?

Support: **Think about how you celebrate birthdays in your family. Tell me about your last birthday.** Share a story about something you like to do on your birthday. Invite children to share their stories.

More to Learn

My Birthday Story
Have children draw their own birthday pictures. Write down each child's short birthday story to share with the class.

More Stories Like Mine
Ask children to share one thing about themselves. (I like to play soccer.) (I have a baby sister.) Write a list of these characteristics. Take the list on a class trip to the library. Ask the librarian to help find some books about characters with the same traits.

What's Alike?

Make Connections Between Stories

We can better understand stories when we find connections between them. Sometimes connections are as simple as "Both books are about bears" or "Both books have boys in them." However, as children gain experience with this skill, they will see how some characters have similar problems or another deeper commonality. Story connections make for lifelong reading enjoyment.

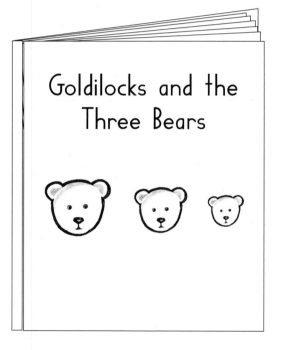

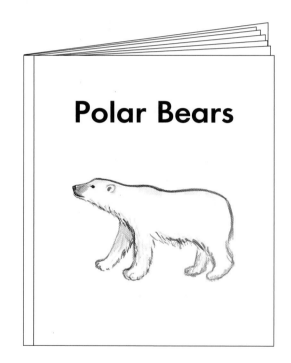

Look What We're Learning

Comprehension
- Describe connections between stories
- Learn about a topic and relate it to real life
- Explain how a story connects to personal experience

Oral Language
- Share opinions and ideas in conversation and discussion

Vocabulary

like

same

What's Alike?

Materials/Setup:
- *Rainbow Fish* by Marcus Pfister
- *It's Mine!* by Leo Lionni

Grouping:
Small group; Whole class

English Language Learners:
Preview vocabulary words **friend** and **share**. Children can say the words in their home languages if they know them. At this stage of development, they may still be learning their first languages and may not yet know the vocabulary words.

Objective
Children make connections between stories.

Activity
Sometimes stories are alike in some ways. Listen to these two stories and think about how they are the similar.

1. Read *Rainbow Fish*. You may want to read these stories at two different times during the day. **What did Rainbow Fish find out?**

2. Read *It's Mine!* **What did the three frogs find out?**

3. **How were these two stories like each other?** (The characters learned to share.)

4. **What can we do to be good friends who share?**

✓ Check for Understanding

Listen to children's responses to your questions about how the stories are similar. Are they able to make connections between the two stories?

Support: Show two stories that have the same animals as characters such as *Goldilocks and the Three Bears* and *Brown Bear, Brown Bear, What Do You See?* Talk about how the animals look or behave alike.

More to Learn

Tell a Connecting Story
After reading a favorite story, have children draw another character. **What could your character do the same as the characters in the story we just read? What do you do the same as the characters?**

Connections Match
For a challenge, display books that the class has read that connect in some way to each other. Have children choose two books and say why they connect. Ask them to also choose a book that relates to them.

You Caught Me!

Retell a Story

When children retell stories, we get a clear picture of whether they have understood them. Retelling also helps to process memories and organize thoughts. It is a key part of lasting comprehension.

Look What We're Learning

Comprehension
- Retell story or event with pictures
- Order the events of a story correctly using pictures
- Listen to learn what happened in a story
- Enjoy books and reading activities

Oral Language
- Demonstrate active listening by attending to stories and instruction
- Talk about experiences and observations with words

You Caught Me!

Materials/Setup:
- Children's fairy tale or folk tale

Grouping:
Small group; Whole class

English Language Learners:
Use the Line It Up™ Story Cards. Give the three cards from one story to three children. Have them put themselves in the correct order and sit down. Have each of the children say what is happening on their card.

Objective
Children retell a story with pictures.

Activity
First, I'll read the story. Then I'll try to say it in my own words. Please listen carefully in case I need your help.

1. Read a familiar story to the group.

2. **Now I'm going to tell you the story again without reading the words. Listen to see if I get it right. If I say something wrong, tell me by saying, "Nooooo!"**

3. As you retell the story, change certain characters or settings along the way. For example, Little Red Riding Hood walked through the football field, or the three little pigs were afraid of the big bad dinosaur.

4. Every time children catch you, say, **Oh, you caught me! What really happens next?** Ask one child to say that part the right way. Encourage the child to show the picture from the book.

✓ Check for Understanding
Invite several children to tell the story the "right" way. Observe their retellings. Some children may be more comfortable retelling the story with you privately. Can they retell the story?

Support: Put up the Line It Up Story Cards for "Little Miss Muffet." Tell the nursery rhyme with a mistake. Say, **Little Miss Muffet sat on a tuffet eating her curds and whey. Along came a lion and sat down beside her.** Have children say, "Nooooo, it's a spider."

More to Learn

Retell and Re-enact
Read a different story, have children retell the story and then act out parts of the story.

Sing, Say, and Act
Play "Dumplin' Song," track 27 on the *Sing, Sound & Count With Me* CD. Assign children or groups of children to sing, retell, and act out the different parts in the song.

Listening for Information

Find Facts

In addition to stories, we can read informational books. Children learn to listen for those facts and begin to understand that fiction and nonfiction are two different types of reading material. Strategies used for each type of reading will benefit children later in school and throughout their lives.

Look What We're Learning

Comprehension

- Generate a list of facts from an informational text
- Participate in a discussion restating facts about the topic of an informational text
- Listen to gain and share information

Oral Language

- Learn new words linked to content being taught
- Use new words linked to content being taught
- Talk about experiences and observations with words

Vocabulary

facts

Listening for Information

Materials/Setup:
- Line It Up™ Story Cards, "Growing Pumpkins"

Grouping:
Small group; Whole class

English Language Learners:
Point to one picture and repeat one piece of information in a sentence. Have children repeat the sentence. Invite them to add any additional information they remember and can say out loud to the group. Say the information in short sentences and have them repeat.

Objective
Children generate a list of facts from an informational text.

Activity
I'm going to read something different today. It tells us lots of information about pumpkins. See if you can remember some of the information after I'm done.

1. Read "Growing Pumpkins" aloud to the class.

2. As you read the selection again, stop after each card and ask what information they heard. Make a list of brief facts stated by the children.

3. At the end, show the pictures again. Ask children to say a fact related to each picture.

✓ Check for Understanding
Choose an informational book about an animal. Have children name facts from this text. Are they giving information when they share?

Support: Show a short nature video. Have children name a fact from the video.

More to Learn

Our Own Book
Have children create artwork related to an informational text. Each creation should depict one of the facts that they learned. Compile their artwork into a class version of the text. Have children narrate as you show their pictures.

We're the Experts
After a field trip or completing a learning unit, have each child tell you a fact. Create a list of facts from the experience. Have each child act out one fact.

We Belong Together

Sort Information

Categorizing is way of grouping things and is a critical thinking skill for organizing information. Children sort objects by color, size, and shape. They can also sort information by topic. Children figure out what belongs in the same group as they build valuable thinking skills.

Eats Meat

Tyrannosaurus Rex

Allosaurus

Eats Plants

Scolosaurus

Triceratops

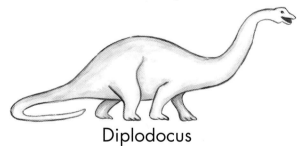

Diplodocus

Look What We're Learning

Comprehension

- Categorize topics from informational text by commonality
- Describe a topic after listening to an informational text
- Make comparisons based on information in informational texts

Social-Emotional

- Take turns with peers

Vocabulary

category

We Belong Together

Materials/Setup:
- Children's book about dinosaurs
- Plastic dinosaurs

Grouping:
Small group; Whole class

English Language Learners:
Preview the two categories to make sure children know the difference. Have children repeat the categories as they place the dinosaur or bird in the appropriate group. (This dinosaur eats meat. This dinosaur eats plants.) Ask for volunteers instead of putting children on the spot. They will participate when they are comfortable. Choose ways for them to participate using fewer words and more movement.

Objective
Children categorize information by topic.

Activity
Let's learn some information about dinosaurs. It will help us put our dinosaurs into groups.

1. Read a dinosaur book to the group.

2. **What did the book tell us about what dinosaurs eat?** If children need assistance, re-read the pages that talk about dinosaurs' diet.

3. **Let's put our dinosaurs in groups by what they eat. We'll put the meat-eating dinosaurs in one group and the plant-eating ones in the other group.**

4. **How do we know which dinosaurs eat meat and which ones eat plants?** If children need help, re-read the pages that give the information.

5. Have children take turns placing each dinosaur with the correct group using the information from the text.

✓ Check for Understanding

Read another informational text about birds. Have children group the birds by ability to fly. Re-read information as needed to help children sort. Are children able to sort by category?

Support: Have children sort farm animals from dinosaurs.

More to Learn

They're Good for You
Show a book about healthful foods. Have children cut out magazine pictures of fruits and vegetables. Let children create a poster with fruit on one side and vegetables on the other. Have fun categorizing and comparing fruits and vegetables. If children need help, re-read the information.

Musical Instruments
Read an informational book on musical instruments. Talk about the groups of instruments: brass, woodwinds, strings, and percussion. For more of a challenge, have children listen to instruments from each group. Then let them try to pick the group from recordings of instruments.

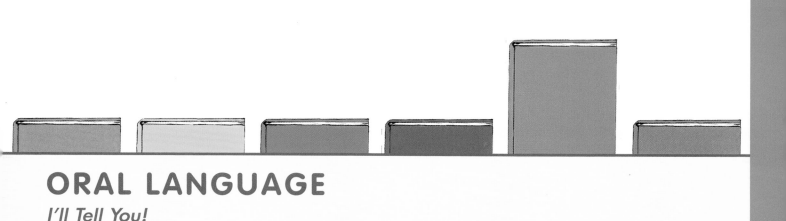

ORAL LANGUAGE
I'll Tell You!

Young children are exposed to conversations and language in many settings. This allows them to develop both the ability to listen and receive language and to generate and communicate language. Oral language is necessary for us to effectively communicate our opinions, thoughts, and ideas. It is also the foundation of literacy development.

Oral language is simply children's ability to listen and express themselves. Pre-K children learn to understand and use language to express their feelings, thoughts, and observations. These skills are key to the development of reading and writing skills. Children develop oral language skills through observation and interaction. They experiment with new vocabulary words and develop oral language skills by listening to, retelling, and narrating stories. Young children love to participate in dramatic play and act out situations that communicate their thoughts, feelings, ideas, and experiences.

The activities in this domain help children learn to:
- **Ask and Respond to Questions**
- **Follow Directions**
- **Talk About Feelings**
- **Talk About Experiences**
- **Learn New Words**
- **Use Manners**
- **Use Words that Describe**
- **Tell a Story**

Below is the significant research for this domain. For additional Oral Language resources, see the reference section at the end of this teacher's guide.

Silverman, R., and J. Crandell. 2010. "Vocabulary Practices in Prekindergarten and Kindergarten Classrooms." *Reading Research Quarterly* 45(3):318-340.

Snow, C.E., P. Tabors, P. Nicholson, and B. Kirkland. 1995. "SHELL: Oral Language and Early Literacy Skills in Kindergarten and First-Grade Children." *Journal of Research in Childhood Education* 10:37-48.

Storch, S. A., G. J. Whitehurst. 2002. "Oral Language and Code-Related Precursors to Reading: Evidence from a Longitudinal Structural Model." *Developmental Psychology* 38:934-947.

Word Time™

Word Time boosts Pre-K children's vocabulary, thinking, and speaking skills through participation in friendly, active lessons. Because these skills are so essential, Word Time has its own dedicated teacher's guide. Word Time includes:

- Teacher's guide
  - Includes 48 weeks of lessons, organized into 12 instructional themes
- 295 Easy-to-read laminated Word Cards
  - Promote left-to-right visual tracking
  - Numbered by lesson and labeled by block so they are easy to find and file
- Squawker, the parrot puppet
  - Helps you teach daily vocabulary including prepositions, verbs, adjectives, and nouns

Squawker

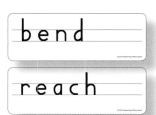

You'll like it because . . .

Word Time is a fun and easy way to build strong vocabulary, promote print awareness, and build grammar skills. Children learn words and their meanings, practice using them in sentences, and apply them in conversation. Word Time is organized by days of the week. Mondays are for action sentences (verbs), Wednesdays for describing sentences (adjectives), and Fridays for questions and answers (nouns). Tuesdays and Thursdays are for optional educational activities.

Squawker the parrot is more than a puppet, he's your teaching assistant. He engages children in saying words and sentences and starts conversations to help students share their personal experiences. Parents can also use Squawker at home to extend their children's learning experience and develop their child's oral language skills.

 Go to A Click Away to download a printable version of Squawker.

Where you'll see it

Alphabet Knowledge	**Oral Language**
Concepts About Print	**Writing**

© 2011 Get Set for School®

Discovery Teaching in Your Day

Oral Language

Old Favorites

Act It Out: When you teach action verbs (e.g., walk, skip), have children act out the word. Use a multisensory approach that allows them to see, hear, touch, and feel the meaning behind a word. Review action verbs by dividing the class into two groups. Say a word to one group. Have children in that group act out the verb while the other group guesses.

Picture Displays: Introduce nouns with a picture of a person, place, or thing. When you have introduced the word, paste the picture to a sheet of paper and write the word beneath. Display the pictures on a wall or in a class word book.

Class Word Book: Keep a list of words for review. Make a page for each word. Children can add illustrations. Place each page in a binder for children to review and share with others. You can alphabetize the pages to subtly introduce dictionary skills.

Have You Tried These?

Make the Most of Read-Alouds: Skim your read-aloud book. Which words are unfamiliar? Are these words that children will use again? Can they use the illustrations to learn the meaning of the words? Choose two to three words from your book to introduce before reading. Use them in conversation after reading and throughout the week. Keep them on a list for review.

Stretch It: When deeply exploring a subject (e.g., bugs) you will find that children are able to learn more challenging vocabulary. Their curiosity will motivate them to seek out and remember more specific words (e.g., insect, caterpillar). They may also learn words well beyond their grade level (e.g., exoskeleton).

Mix in Some Get Set for School® Activities

A favorite Get Set for School product for developing oral language is Word Time™. The lessons follow monthly themes: Social behavior, School, My Body, Sky, Animals, Work, Health, Earth, etc. Themes become familiar, which helps children remember and talk about subjects. You can also use Squawker, the parrot puppet, by placing him in new places all around the classroom. He's never in the same place. Children then find him and say, "Squawker is on the chair," or "Squawker is near the blocks."

It's so much fun to look for Squawker. When children say where he is, they're learning to use prepositions (in, under, between, beside, near, in front of, etc.) and prepositional phrases (under the table) naturally and accurately. They're also speaking in complete sentences, but to children, they're just helping to locate Squawker. Whether they're talking about where he is or talking to him, they're talking. Squawker loves to talk too and when he does, he boosts your children's oral language skills.

Ask & Tell

Ask & Respond to Questions

Oral language develops naturally. Babies and children listen and understand language (receptive vocabulary) before they use language (expressive vocabulary). Provide young children many opportunities to participate in everyday conversations through listening and sharing. At first, children use language to say what they need or want ("More juice!"). Soon after, they begin to share their thoughts and ideas. Ask questions to encourage participation in class discussions and to foster language skills.

Ask & Tell:
Tune: The Farmer and the Dell

Teacher - What color is the sky? What color is the sky?
I really want to know, what color is the sky?

Children - The sky is _____. The sky is _____.
We really want to tell you that the sky is _____.

Other verses to sing:

What is your name?
Who is your teacher?
When do you sleep?
Where is the door?
What is the weather?

Look What We're Learning

Oral Language
- Ask and respond to simple questions:
  Who? What? When? Where?
- Speak in complete sentences made up of three or more words

Social-Emotional
- Cooperate with other children

Materials/Setup:
• "Ask & Tell" lyrics

Grouping:
Small group; Whole class

English Language Learners:
Preview the song used in the activity. Use hand gestures and pictures to help children understand the vocabulary.

Objective
Children ask and respond to simple questions.

Activity
Let's have fun and sing "Ask & Tell."

1. Have children sit in a circle to sing "Ask & Tell."
2. Sing the first question. Then lead the children in singing the response.
3. Continue until four to five questions are completed.
4. When children are ready, let them volunteer to sing a question.
5. You can start out by singing as a class. As children are ready, ask more personal questions.

✓ Check for Understanding

Observe children ask and answer questions. What questions do they ask? Do they answer in complete sentences?

Support: Focus on one type of "W" question at a time. Ask children **Where are the blocks? Where are the cars? Where are the _____?** Have the children move to the answer.

More to Learn

All About Me
Feature different children each week to learn more about them. Encourage them to ask who, where, when, what, and why questions about their friend, e.g., **What is your favorite food?**

Who Am I?
Read *Mat Man Hats.* Help children ask and answer questions. **Who delivers the mail?** (The mail carrier delivers the mail.) **Who flies the plane?** (The pilot flies the plane.) **Who fights the fires?** (The firefighter fights the fires.) **Who bakes the cake?** (The baker bakes the cake.)

Follow Me

Follow Directions

It is important that children follow directions outside of the classroom. When children practice following directions they can better understand the purpose and importance of directions. They can also understand what can happen when they don't follow directions correctly.

19. TAP, TAP, TAP

Tap, tap, tap big lines
Tap big lines together. (Repeat 1X)
Tap a little louder now
Tap along with me
Tap a little softer now
Tap along with me

Tap, tap, tap big lines
Tap them on the floor (Repeat 1X)
Play your big lines like a drum
Play along with me
Play your big lines like a drum
Play along with me

Touch, touch, touch big lines
Touch them to your toes
Touch, touch, touch big lines
Touch them to your nose
Touch them on your shoulders now
Don't forget your head
Touch them right down to your knees
And everybody sneeze… ACHOO!

Move, move, move big lines
Move them in the air
Move, move, move big lines
Move them under your chair
Move your big lines to the front
Move them to the back
Move your big lines to the side
Now put them in your lap

Tap, tap, tap big lines
Tap them at the top
Tap, tap, tap big lines
Tap 'til I say STOP
(Tap 11X) STOP; (Repeat 3X)
Now let's try it faster!
(Tap 11X) STOP; (Repeat 3X)

20. GOLDEN SLIPPERS (INSTRUMENTAL)

Look What We're Learning

Oral Language
- Listen to follow directions (up to three or four steps)
- Complete a task by following oral directions (up to three steps)

Comprehension
- Listen to perform a task

Social-Emotional
- Imitate teacher's body movements

Materials/Setup:
- Wood Pieces
  – Big Lines (two per child)
- *Get Set for School Sing Along* CD, track 19, "Tap, Tap, Tap"

Grouping:
Small group; Whole class

English Language Learners:
Preview the song used in the activity. Use hand gestures and pictures to help children understand the vocabulary.

Objective
Children listen to follow directions.

Activity
We're going to have fun tapping Big Lines. Follow me.

1. Give each child two Big Lines.
2. Play "Tap, Tap, Tap."
3. Children follow as you move to the directions of the song.
4. Alternative: Sing **If you're following directions and you know it, clap your hands.** Lead the children through a variety of different actions (e.g., pat your knees, turn around, etc.) they can do to show they are following directions.

✓ Check for Understanding

When you are done, play a game of "Listen and Wait." Tell children to listen for their turn. Say, **My turn.** Then tap Big Lines three times. Say, **Your turn.** Children tap Big Lines three times. Vary the number of taps to make the activity more challenging. Observe children. Are they following directions?

Support: Use some of our other songs. In Get Set for School® Readiness & Writing program, we also use the *Rock, Rap, Tap & Learn* CD. "Counting at the Table" and "It's Line Up Time" on the *Sing, Sound & Count With Me* CD are great songs to teach children to follow directions.

More to Learn

Follow the Dance
Help the children do the Hokie Pokie and watch as they follow directions.

Directions to the Treasure
Have children go on a scavenger hunt. Hide paper items in the classroom. Items could be hearts for Valentine's Day or shamrocks for St. Patrick's Day. Have groups of three children follow your directions to find the items.

How Does It Feel?

Talk About Feelings

Feelings are responses to situations in our lives. Young children may struggle to identify their feelings and the feelings of others. They may also struggle to express how they feel with words. When they can identify and communicate feelings, children can deal with their feelings more constructively and can develop emotionally.

Look What We're Learning

Oral Language
- Communicate feelings with words
- Communicate thoughts with words

Social-Emotional
- Name feelings he or she is experiencing
- Name emotions experienced by others

Materials/Setup:
- Craft sticks
- Tape
- *Sing, Sound & Count With Me* CD, track 8, "Smile!"
- Feeling Faces cutouts (one per child)

Grouping:
Small group; Whole class

English Language Learners:
Help children find pictures of people in a magazine showing a particular emotion. Help them cut out the pictures and make a collage. Talk about the emotions shown in the pictures.

Objective
Children communicate thoughts and feelings with words.

Activity
We are going to sing a fun song called "Smile!"

1. Prepare a smiley Feeling Face cutout on a craft stick—one per child.
2. Play "Smile!"
3. Children hold up their sticks when they hear the word, "smile."
4. **The song talks about being happy, scared, mad, and sad. Being happy, scared, mad, and sad are all feelings that we may have.**
5. Talk about other feelings. Pretend to have other feelings. Draw a symbol on the board for each one. **It is okay to have all of those feelings. When you are mad, you can say that you feel mad, but it is not okay to hit someone because you are mad.**

✓ Check for Understanding
Observe children as they interact with others throughout their day. Are children communicating their emotions?

Support: Make a happy face and say, **I'm happy!** Children move Big or Little Curves from Wood Pieces to show happy and say, "I'm happy!" Make a sad face and say, **I'm sad!** Children move Big or Little Curves to show sad and say, "I'm sad!"

More to Learn

Feelings Talk
Talk about each emotion and ask children to share an example of when they felt the emotion.

Book of Emotions
Read a book that displays the character(s) feeling different emotions. Help children identify the emotions as you read.

Reach & Tell

Talk About Experiences

Children learn from their experiences as they see new things and gain knowledge. When they share their experiences and observations, other children learn too. Communication also helps children process their thoughts. When they talk about experiences and observations, they receive confirmation and/or guidance to develop their thinking further. Communication about experiences and observations can also be important for safety. This skill is critical for both developmental and practical reasons.

Look What We're Learning

Oral Language
- Talk about experiences and observations with words
- Communicate thoughts with words
- Use words to describe an object or a person's traits
- Speak in complete sentences made up of three or more words

Reach & Tell

Materials/Setup:
- Sound Around Box™:
  - Picture Tiles

Grouping:
Small group; Whole class

English Language Learners:
Show children selected pictures of simple activities. Help them show and say what is happening in the picture.

Objective
Children talk about experiences and observations with words.

Activity
We are going to reach in our Sound Around Box and choose a picture to talk about.

1. Invite a child to pull out a Picture Tile from the Sound Around Box.

2. Show the class.

3. Children take turns talking about an experience they had or something they observed about the item, e.g., if they select a picture of a backpack, children may say, "I have a red backpack. This is how I put it on my back. I put in my arm. I put in my other arm."

4. Help children communicate their experiences if needed. Encourage them to speak in complete sentences.

✓ Check for Understanding

Observe as children say something they have experienced related to the selected tile. What words do they use to describe what happened?

Support: Show a Line It Up™ Coloring Card. Talk about what's on the card. Use the conversation starters to encourage children to share their own experiences.

More to Learn

School Trip
Take the children on a field trip around the school to observe what people are doing. Have them come back to the classroom and share something they observed.

What's Your Experience?
Have children tell you about an experience they had or observations they've made at the zoo, park, circus, a birthday party, their grandma's house, etc.

© 2011 Get Set for School®

Reach & Tell **141**

What's the Word?

Learn New Words

Vocabulary is the collection of words we know and understand. Vocabulary development is essential for overall reading success. A rich vocabulary greatly supports children's ability to comprehend what they read. Game playing is a fun, interactive way to increase vocabulary.

Look What We're Learning

Oral Language
- Learn words linked to content being taught
- Use new words linked to content being taught
- Communicate thoughts with words
- Talk about experiences and observations with words

What's the Word?

Materials/Setup:
- Sound Around Box™
- Objects to teach vocabulary

Grouping:
Small group; Whole class

English Language Learners:
Preview pictures and props to help children understand the words. Say each word and have the children repeat. Using props that children can manipulate and hold will bring the words to life.

Objective
Children learn new words.

Activity
Let's go on an expedition for new words. Our Sound Around Box is an underwater treasure chest. Let's explore and see what we find.

1. Gather items or pictures that show your vocabulary words—about two to three. Put them in the Sound Around Box.

2. **Who wants to explore the treasure chest? Show us what you found. What is it?** Have child name the item or allow the class to answer. Help as needed.

3. **Have you ever seen this before? What can you tell me about it?** Encourage children to share their experiences and describe what they see.

4. Write the word on the side of the Sound Around Box.

5. Repeat Steps 2–3 until all items are explored.

✓ Check for Understanding

Observe children as they talk about the items. Do they understand what the words mean?

Support: Have children help you pack the treasure chest. Talk about each item as you place it in the chest to prepare them for the new vocabulary.

More to Learn

Vocabulary Fishing
Place pictures of people, places, or things in Sound Around Box. Have children fish out a picture and say a sentence about it. (The umbrella is red.)

What Am I?
Use two or three facts to describe a person, place, or thing. **I am furry and I bark. What am I?**
After children guess, introduce the vocabulary words: dog, bark, furry, etc.

Manners in Action

Use Manners

Children begin to learn manners at an early age. They learn socially acceptable behavior that allows them to interact well with others. Good manners create a positive environment that encourage others to reciprocate. It also creates a foundation of mutual respect with those around them.

Look What We're Learning

Oral Language
- Use manners
- Listen to follow directions
- Speak in complete sentences made up of three or more words

Social-Emotional
- Cooperate with other children
- Participate in imaginary and dramatic play
- Take turns with peers

Vocabulary

manners

Manners in Action

Materials/Setup:
- Play dinner items (food, plates cups, etc.)

Grouping:
Small group; Whole class

English Language Learners:
Greetings can be unique to a culture. Get to know your students so that you can be sensitive to how they greet one another in their homes. Help them learn manners by modeling and providing opportunities where they can use their new skills.

Objective
Children follow rules and use manners in conversation.

Activity
We're going to learn table manners.

1. Invite children to have a pretend dinner with you. Tell them, **Thank you for coming. Please sit down.**

2. Begin passing serving dishes. **Would you like some <u>salad</u>?** Help the next child respond with "Yes, please" or "No, thank you." The child pretends to serve himself, then turns to his neighbor and repeats the offer. Continue passing the item until everyone has had a chance. Remind children to wait until everyone is served before eating.

3. Pretend to eat. Model how to ask for something. **May I have the salt, please?** Say, **Thank you**, when the item is passed to you. The passing child should respond, "You're welcome."

4. Demonstrate saying, **Thank you for dinner. May I please be excused?** when you leave the table.

5. Continue to practice table manners by repeating this activity with table groups at snack time.

✓ Check for Understanding

Observe children as they say "Please" and "Thank You" at the dinner table. Observe them using manners throughout the day— on the playground, during free play, etc.

Support: First, demonstrate with one child. Have child hold a paper plate.
Ask, **Please, may I have the plate?** He passes the plate. Say, **Thank you.**
Then it's the child's turn to ask for the plate and to say "Thank you." Children work in pairs passing the plate back and forth with manners.

More to Learn

Manners Relay
Have children form a line. Place a tray of items and a plate at the front of the line. The first child chooses an item and places it on the plate. Each child in line must use good manners to receive the item before continuing. Continue until everyone has had a turn at the front.

A Special Thanks
Help the children write a thank you note. They can cut out a picture to glue to the card, or they can draw a picture. Help them write "Thank you for <u>the gift</u>" and sign the card. Their signatures can be just the first letter of their names.

Touch or Look

Use Words that Describe

The use of descriptive language is a crucial part of a young child's language development. Descriptive words describe people, places, or things. Descriptive language gives additional information about a subject, identifying people or things, communicating emotions, or understanding situations. Children learn to describe in simple, complete sentences. For example: The dog is furry. The ball is round.

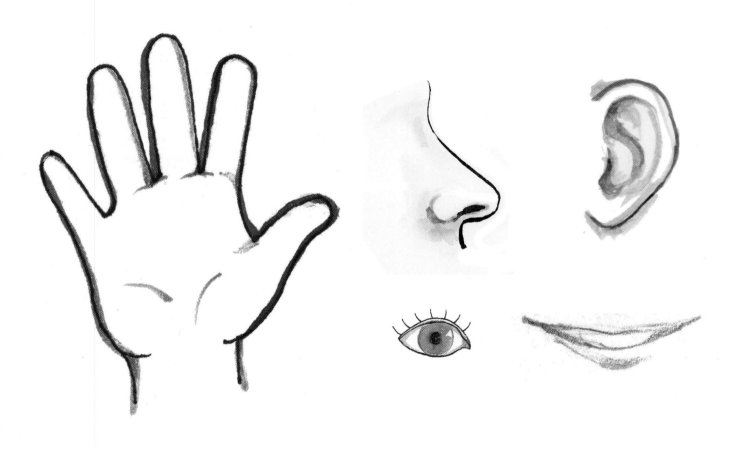

Look What We're Learning

Oral Language
- Use words to describe an object or a person's traits
- Talk about experiences and observations with words
- Communicate thoughts with words

Writing
- Understand there is a way to write that conveys meaning.

Vocabulary

describe

Materials/Setup:
- Sound Around Box™
- Teddy bear, baseball, dough (all in separate brown bags)
- Colorful shirt, baseball, pipe cleaner

Grouping:
Small group; Whole class

English Language Learners:
Talk about the five senses one at a time over a period of time. Review some of the words that are connected to a given sense—sour, sweet, spicy, for taste. Use real items to further explain each sense. For example, have children taste lemon juice and sugar.

Objective
Children use words to describe an object or a person's traits.

Activity
Our fingers and eyes tell us about things. When we use these, we are using our senses. When I call you, tell me if you want to touch or look at something in the Sound Around Box.

1. Select a child and ask her, **Touch or look?**

2. If child says "touch," allow her to reach into the box. If she says "look," pull an item out for her to look at.

3. Say to the child, **What is it? What does it feel (look) like?**

4. Write child's descriptive words on the side of the Sound Around Box.

5. Repeat 1–4 with all items in the box.

6. Point and read written words on the side of the box.

✓ Check for Understanding

Observe children describing objects. Are they using their senses to help them? Are they using the descriptive vocabulary they have learned?

Support: Help children compare two objects using descriptive words. For example, compare a pen and pencil. **The pencil is yellow. The pen is black. The pencil is longer than the pen.** Think of using descriptors from the different senses. Make it accessible to children whose senses may be limited in some way.

More to Learn

Taste or Smell
Repeat activity using items that a child can taste or smell. Place items on the table and use an easel to write descriptive words.

Silly Sentences
Choose a familiar object. Help children create a list of words that describe the object. For silly fun, apply the same words to another object. (The backpack is furry and says meow.)

Tell Me About It

Tell a Story

Narrative or storytelling skills are essential to a young child's literacy development. Being able to tell a story or recount events demonstrates comprehension of what is read or seen. The more a young child practices narrating a story, the easier it becomes. This skill is useful for reading comprehension, and for describing a real event. It can also be very enjoyable for the storyteller. Acting out a story is an excellent way for children to remember and retell a story.

Look What We're Learning

Oral Language
- Describe everyday routines and events
- Tell stories
- Talk about experiences and observations with words
- Speak in complete sentences made up of three or more words

Materials/Setup:
- Large 8" x 10" child friendly photos
- Line It Up™ Magnetic Bar

Grouping:
Small group; Whole class

English Language Learners:
Create your own picture stories with your students starring in the story. Help them tell you what is happening in the story.

Objective
Children tell stories and describe everyday, routine events.

Activity
It's story time. Let's talk about some pictures.

1. Hang up the first picture in the Line It Up Bar. **What do you see?**

2. Encourage children to share their own experiences that connect with the picture.

3. Help children communicate their thoughts and tell their stories. Model and ask questions.

4. Repeat with other pictures.

✓ Check for Understanding

Observe children telling stories. Are they able to describe everyday routines and events? Do they provide details?

Support: Have children use props to tell and act out their events or stories.

More to Learn

It Happens Every Day
Have children tell you about an everyday event. They can talk about how they get ready in the morning, how they help someone cook, etc.

The End?
Give children different story scenarios and have them act out the end. It would be fun to give outrageous scenarios as well. **What would happen if someone gave you a bicycle? If you went to the beach? If you saw a lion on the street?**

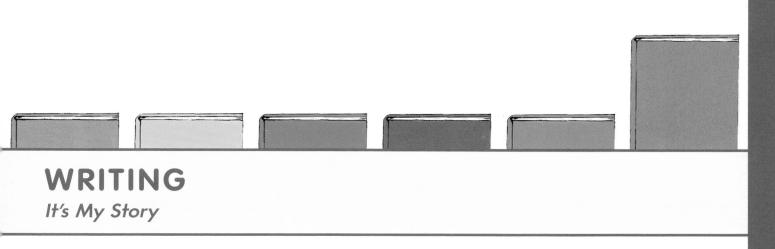

WRITING
It's My Story

Young children recognize the importance of writing. They want to make sense of what they see and be just like grown-ups. In Pre-K, most children are just beginning to learn about letters and are eager to start writing the letters in their first and last names. Although they may only have limited handwriting ability, they are ready to share their thoughts and ideas with their friends, teachers, and families.

Pre-K children are ready to identify the difference between pictures and print, retell stories using their own words or through dramatic play, and communicate their ideas to be written down. They can scribble "words" and draw pictures that express their ideas. Children learn that there is meaning in the words they read and that there is meaning in the words they say and have written. When you think about writing for Pre-K children, story creation, and sentence writing probably do not come to mind. Young children enjoy creating stories and seeing their words become print. You are the scribe, and the children are the masterminds.

Children learn about how writing is done by watching their parents and teachers write. Pre-K children are ready for pre-writing and beginning handwriting. Use the Get Set for School® Readiness & Writing program for beginning handwriting instruction.

The activities in this domain help children learn to:

- **Represent Events in a Story**
- **Retell Through Play**
- **Dictate Information**
- **Label Objects**
- **Share Ideas**
- **Make a Topic Choice**

Below is the significant research for this domain. For additional Writing resources, see the reference section at the end of this teacher's guide.

Berninger V. W., R. D. Abbott, J. Jones, B.J. Wolf, L. Gould, and A. Anderson-Youngstrom. 2006. "Early Development of Language by Hand: Composing, Reading, Listening, and Speaking Connections; Three Letter-Writing Modes; and Fast Mapping in Spelling." *Developmental Neuropsychology* 29:61-92.

Schickedanz, J.A., and R.M. Casbergue. 2004. *Writing in Preschool: Learning to Orchestrate Meaning and Marks.* Newark, DE: International Reading Association.

Wasik, B. A. 2010. "What Teachers Can Do to Promote Preschoolers' Vocabulary Development: Strategies from an Effective Language and Literacy Professional Development Coaching Model." *The Reading Teacher* 63(8):621-633.

Line It Up™

Line It Up Coloring Cards engage children with active lessons that promote early literacy and motor skills. The Line It Up Coloring Cards set includes:

- 26 Coloring Cards
  - Black and white illustrations to color
  - Wipe-off surface that works with dry erase crayons
- Activity booklet
  - Conversation starters for every coloring card
- Line It Up Bar
  - Unique display bar that holds cards in place while allowing children to place cards in, out, and around the bar

You'll like them because . . .

Line It Up Coloring Cards are a perfect way to encourage good writing habits. The cards fit into a bar to create a vertical drawing surface. This promotes good wrist positioning and helps children build strength in the shoulders and arms. The Coloring Cards feature the black and white illustrations from the *My First School Book* activity book. They invite conversation, personalization and creativity. Use activities in this teacher's guide, the Line It Up activity booklet, or create your own great ideas to make the most of the Line It Up Coloring Cards.

Where you'll see them

Phonological Awareness

Oral Language

Writing

Discovery Teaching in Your Day

Writing

Old Favorites

Bring in the Toys: Children benefit from expressing their creative ideas through play. Provide stuffed toys and props to allow them to act out stories. When celebrating themes, provide props and help children with dramatic play.

Labels, Labels, Labels: Allow children to find things of interest to them in the classroom. Once the item is discussed, give a child a label to place on the item. With this activity, children build a rich vocabulary and learn to associate print with pictures and objects.

Have You Tried These?

Class Journal: After a shared event, such as a field trip, a special visitor, or a school celebration, have children share their impressions. Guide them to say complete sentences. Write the sentences down, word for word. Add a title and date. Have children draw pictures of their experiences.

Science Labels: As the class shares science observations (e.g., birds building a nest or a classroom butterfly nursery), have children draw the changes each day or every few days. Have children dictate labels by their pictures. Write these at places designated for each child.

Mix in Some Get Set for School® Activities

That's My Favorite: Use *My Book* to have children draw and discuss their favorite things. They can draw their favorite food and tell you a story. Ask each of the children to tell you about their pictures. Write the exact words across the top or bottom of the drawing. Read it back to them so they know that what they said has been recorded on the paper.

From Color to Conversation: Use Line It Up™ Coloring Cards to prompt conversations about topics that lead to stories. Children can draw their ideas on the cards and share them as a class.

Replay Robins

Represent Events in a Story

Children love to hear favorite stories repeatedly. When you provide stuffed animals or other play figures, you help bring familiar stories to life so that children can practice the rhythm and structure of storytelling. They are naturally creative, so they will extend the story and add details during play. With this activity, you are building the foundation for future written stories.

Look What We're Learning

Writing
- Recognize that stories can be documented through pictures and play

Comprehension
- Identify the beginning, middle, and end of a story
- Order the events of a story correctly using pictures
- Re-enact a story or event

Oral Language
- Use new words linked to content being taught
- Tell stories

Social-Emotional
- Cooperate with other children
- Participate in imaginary and dramatic play
- Take turns

Replay Robins

Materials/Setup:
- Line It Up™:
  - "Ready for Robins" Story Cards
  - Magnetic Bar
- Stuffed toy birds
- Toy eggs
- Blocks, baskets, or other classroom play materials

Grouping:
Pairs

English Language Learners:
Let children retell the story using props to show what they understand. Describe their actions in short sentences and have them repeat the sentences back.

Objective
Children retell a story using classroom play materials.

Activity
After we read a story, you can retell it your own way.

1. Read "Ready for Robins."

2. Share the blocks, baskets, or other play materials. **Can you make a home for the birds?**

3. Invite each child to play with one of the parent birds. They may begin to play and interact without support. If not, ask questions to help them get started. **What could the parents say to each other? What will they do next?** Encourage them to speak for the birds, creating dialogue.

4. Have children add eggs, other birds, etc. to continue the story.

5. Encourage children to play out the whole story and to continue until play naturally ends.

✓ Check for Understanding
Observe children as they act out a story. Are children using language to describe what is happening in the story? Are they telling the story with words, play, or both?

Support: Play along with children. Use another toy bird to ask questions that encourage participation. **Have you seen any sticks? We need sticks for our nest.**

More to Learn

Add a Character
If children can easily retell the story and add dialogue, add an unexpected character to the robin's nest (e.g., squirrel, Squawker). Let children adapt the story around this new character.

Character Change
Provide other stuffed animals for children to use for their stories. **What would the story be like with a bear family instead of birds?** Help children find playthings that could be used to make a home for bears.

Hat Play

Retell Through Play

Dramatic play is one of the earliest ways in which young children develop stories. Play allows them to take on different roles and see the world from a new point of view.

Use dramatic play to stimulate children's creativity in preparation for later writing. They are actively telling a story in three dimensions. They plan characters and a setting as well as problems and solutions.

Look What We're Learning

Writing
- Recognize that stories and events can be documented in print, pictures, and play

Oral Language
- Use words linked to content being taught
- Share opinions and ideas in conversation and discussion

Social-Emotional
- Take turns
- Work together to solve a problem
- Participate in imaginary and dramatic play

Materials/Setup:

- *Mat Man Hats*

- Props for various professions, for example, tools for a builder, kitchen utensils for a chef or baker

Grouping:

Small group

English Language Learners:

Help children describe what they are doing when they play with props, for example, "I hammer."

Objective

Children tell a story through dramatic play.

Activity

This week we are going to act out a story.

1. On the first day, read *Mat Man Hats*. Share favorite jobs from the book. Select a favorite for dramatic play.

2. On the second day, introduce a few of the props. Show how props can be used. Let children try.

3. On the third day, help children decide on a storyline and select roles. If they are builders, they might build a tree house.

4. Talk about what each person will do before beginning to play.

5. Help children find the things they need to do their jobs as they play. Ask questions to help them decide what to do next.

6. After play ends, talk about what happened. Repeat this play scenario over a few days. Allow children to take on different roles and adjust the storyline to fit their developing understanding of the jobs. Add new props.

✓ Check for Understanding

Observe children as they tell the story through dramatic play. Do they understand the storyline? Do they stick to their roles and follow the plan? How do they use props?

Support: Re-enact a story with a clear storyline. Select a story or nursery rhyme that is very familiar. Invite children to act out the story and help them add more details from their own imagination.

More to Learn

Create a Prop

Encourage children to create their own props. They can use paper, cloth, clay, bags, and more to enhance their play.

Isabel's Birthday

Use "Isabel's Birthday" from Line It Up™ as inspiration to celebrate a birthday. See Explore Dramatic Play on the back of Card 1 for props and ideas.

Class Journal

Dictate Information

When children share their thoughts (dictate) for you to write, they learn so much about written language. They see that written words are separate and that there are spaces between words. They see that words are written from left to right, stay the same, and can be turned into spoken words.

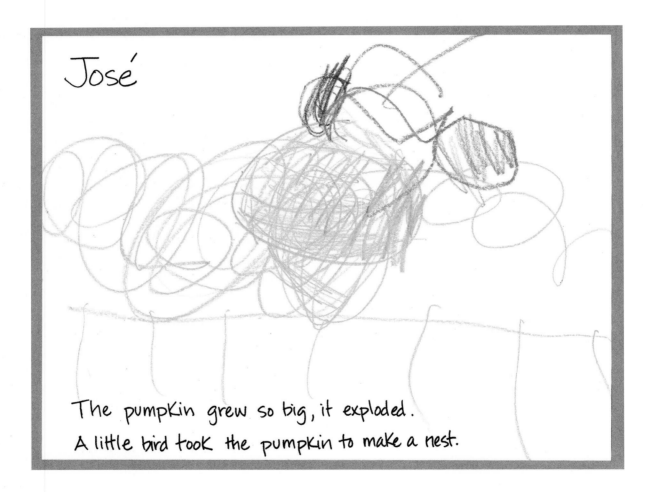

José

The pumpkin grew so big, it exploded.
A little bird took the pumpkin to make a nest.

Look What We're Learning

Writing
- Enjoy writing and engage in writing activities individually or with a group
- Watch teacher write sentences and read them aloud (up to 3)
- Understand there is a way to write that conveys meaning

Oral Language
- Share opinions and ideas in conversation and discussion
- Use new words linked to content being taught

Materials/Setup:

- Line It Up™:
  - "Growing Pumpkins" Story Cards
  - Magnetic Bar
- Paper for each child
- Crayons

Grouping:

Small group; Whole class

English Language Learners:

Bring a real pumpkin for children to see and feel. Write their ideas for them on their papers. Re-read their thoughts as you point to the words.

Objective

Children retell classroom events and stories. They see how the words they say can become written words.

Activity

Today we are going to read a story about pumpkins. When we're done, we are going to draw a picture.

1. Read "Growing Pumpkins."

2. After you read each card, hand it to a child to place on the Line It Up Bar.

3. Discuss the sequence of the story. **What do you think will happen next?**

4. Return to tables and have children draw what happens next.

5. Walk around the room and allow children to share their thoughts. Write what they say on the bottom of their pictures.

6. Put all of their pictures in a class journal to share.

✓ Check for Understanding

Listen and observe children as they talk and draw. What facts do they retell about the story?

Support: Children sometimes need help with their drawings. Ask them what they want to write about and help them start. For example, a child may need you to draw a large circle to start his pumpkin.

More to Learn

Our Classroom Trip

Take a special field trip. Have children retell what they enjoyed about the trip. Record what they say. Journal entries can also be made for other events, such as celebrations, school programs, and so forth.

Explore Writing

Use "Ready for Robins" from Line It Up, using the illustrations to write your own unique class story. See Explore Writing on the back of Card 1 for ideas.

Label the Teacher

Label Objects

Introduce new vocabulary by exposing children to print with pictures. Words used with pictures help children learn to read. Words should be associated with pictures on a daily basis. Children enjoy seeing how words represent pictures and knowing what they say.

Look What We're Learning

Writing
- Dictate labels for objects
- Understand there is a way to write that conveys meaning

Oral Language
- Use new words linked to content being taught

Social-Emotional
- Cooperate with other children
- Take turns

Vocabulary

labels

Label the Teacher

Materials/Setup:
- Paper
- Markers
- Word Time™:
  - 10 cards – head, body, arm, arm, hand, hand, leg, leg, foot, foot

Grouping:
Small group; Whole class

English Language Learners:
Touch your head. **Head.** Have children touch their head and say, "head." Repeat with other body parts.

Objective
Children learn that print can be used to label items.

Activity
Let's have fun labeling.

1. **When you label something you write its name on it. Today we'll label body parts. What is this?** Wave a hand. Write "hand" on a blank label. Continue with other body parts.

2. Lay down or build Mat Man® in center of circle with body part labels in a pile next to you.

3. Select a label helper to choose a label from the pile and show it to you. Read the label. Have the label helper show the label to the class. Read the label together.

4. Have the label helper give the label to another child. Ask the child to place the label beside each body part.

5. Repeat steps 3–4 to label other body parts.

✓ Check for Understanding

Observe children as they say and label body parts. Do they understand where the labels go?

Support: Play Simon Says. **Simon says, Touch your head.** Hold up Word Time card with "head" written on it. Repeat for other body parts or objects around the classroom or school.

More to Learn

Room Label Rhyme
Prepare labels for the floor, wall, and ceiling. **We can label the floor. We can label the wall. But we can't label the ceiling, we're not that tall.** Have children repeat rhyme and label the floor, wall, and ceiling. Label other things in the room.

Explore Science
Use "Growing Pumpkins" from Line It Up™. Allow children to explore the outside and inside of a pumpkin. Label the parts of the pumpkin. See Explore Science on the back of Card 2 for more ideas.

Sign Makers

Share Ideas

Children often want to communicate through writing before their motor skills, alphabet knowledge, and print awareness are fully developed. Encourage this exploration with activities that you can adjust to meet each child's developmental level.

The developmental stages of children's independent writing efforts are well documented. They begin with scribbles, move to letter-like forms, and end with letters. We believe that developmentally appropriate pre-writing instruction is a critical part of this progression. Support your children where they are developmentally, and help them explore the next level.

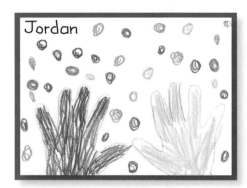

Look What We're Learning

Writing

- Write scribbles, letter-like forms, or actual letters to represent words and ideas
- Hold crayon with proper grip to write
- Use helping hand to stabilize objects and papers
- Understand there is a way to write that conveys meaning
- Share drawings and writing with others

Concepts About Print

- Recognize important signs in our world

Social-Emotional

- Take turns
- Work together to solve a problem

Sign Makers

Materials/Setup:

- Paper
- Flip Crayons®
- Safety and warning signs

Grouping:

Small group

English Language Learners:

To get started, visit the sink. Hands-on experience is the best way to learn. Before making the sign, explain concepts through doing. Say each step as you complete it. For example, **water, soap, rub, rinse, dry.**

Objective

Children use scribbles, pictures, and letters to communicate an idea.

Activity

Signs give information. Let's make our own signs.

1. Begin this activity after talking to children about the importance of washing hands.

2. **There are signs all around us. Some signs warn us of danger. Other signs tell us what to do.** Show sample signs. Share the meaning of each sign.

3. **Signs can have pictures, letters, and words. Show me a sign with pictures. Find a sign with letters.**

4. Move to a table with writing materials. **Let's make signs that tell people to wash their hands. You can use pictures, shapes, letters, or words.**

5. Help children with their signs. It's okay to help spell words if they ask. Think about what they already know and demonstrate some or all of the letters. They may know their letters and be able to produce them as you spell.

6. Encourage children to share their work with the group. Post the signs near a sink.

✓ Check for Understanding

Notice what a child uses to communicate: pictures, scribbles, letters, developmental spelling, etc. Track this development over time. Are they able to convey meaning?

Support: Sing "Crayon Song" from *Get Set for School Sing Along* CD, track 5. Check children's grips and adjust as needed before writing.

More to Learn

Stop and Go

Show children cutouts of blank street signs. Let them guess the signs by the shapes and colors. Show pictures of real signs. Talk about where they might see the signs. Have them choose one and make their own. They will enjoy scribbling and play-writing.

Write and Play

Encourage children to write during play. They can write a letter when playing post office or make a list before playing grocery store. Make writing materials accessible for children to gather on their own.

Just Like You!

Make a Topic Choice

Children make choices all the time: crackers over cookies, swings over the slide, and coloring over their toys. Their reasoning can be matter of fact, make-believe, or a little of both, but they will be sure to tell you about it. Young children also think about what they want to be when they grow up: firemen, doctors, and fairy princesses. Sometimes they just want to be like you. Use this activity to tap into their passions and have them write about it.

Look What We're Learning

Writing
- Choose topics and generate ideas about which to write
- Watch teacher write sentences and read them aloud (up to 3)
- Dictate labels for pictures
- Share drawings and writing with others

Comprehension
- Listen to gain and share information

Oral Language
- Use new words linked to content being taught
- Communicate thoughts with words
- Share opinions and ideas in conversation and discussion

Materials/Setup:

- *Sing Sound & Count With Me* CD, track 29, "Ballet Dancing Truck Driver"
- Paper
- Flip Crayons®
- An easel or dry erase board
- Various clothes and props in the dramatic play area

Grouping:

Small group; Whole class

English Language Learners:

Use pictures to explain different jobs. Teach the words to the children and learn the words in their home languages. Use hand gestures and examples of what other children in the class want to be when they grow up to explain the concept.

Objective

Children think of a topic and write about it.

Activity

Let's listen to a fun song about jobs people like to do.

1. Play "Ballet Dancing Truck Driver" a few times. Encourage children to act out what they hear.

2. **Do you want to be any of the things you heard on the CD or something else? Let's make a list!**

3. Write down children's ideas on an easel or dry erase board.

4. Have children draw what they want to be. Go around, have them dictate what they want to be, and write it for them. (I want to be a fairy when I grow up so I can fly!)

✓ Check for Understanding

Observe children as they draw and say what they want to be when they grow up. Do they make choices about what they want to be? Can they explain their choices and why they made them?

Support: Read books about different jobs or have pictures available for children. You can also ask them what their family members do. This will give them both a visual context and a personal connection for making their choices.

More to Learn

I Choose You

Read a book about a zoo. Invite children to draw a picture of an interesting animal. Ask them to explain why they picked that animal and write what they say. You can also use books about construction, flowers, or places.

Jobs in Our Community

Read and talk about jobs in your community. Ask children what job they might like to have and why. Listen to "That Would Be Me!" track 22 on the *Sing, Sound & Count With Me* CD. Have children tell their job choices in the last verse of the song.

RESOURCES

Language & Literacy Benchmarks

Phonological Awareness

Auditory Discrimination
- Tell whether a sound is an environmental sound or a speech sound
- Identify similarities and differences in sounds
- Tell whether two spoken words are the same or different
- Indicate when a certain sound or word is heard
- Listen to sounds and name objects that make that sound

Rhyming
- Tell whether two spoken words rhyme
- Listen to songs, poems, or nursery rhymes and find the rhymes
- Repeat rhyming words spoken by a teacher
- Produce a word that rhymes with a given word

Segmentation & Syllable Awareness
- Break spoken sentences into words
- Count the number of words in a spoken sentence
- Break compound words apart
- Break words into syllables
- Count the number of syllables in a word (up to 4)
- Break words into two parts: onset and rime

Blending
- Build spoken words into a sentence
- Create a compound word from two familiar words
- Blend syllables into a complete word
- Blend onsets and rimes into a complete word

Alliteration
- Listen to songs, poems, and sentences with words that start with the same sound
- Identify the repeated initial sound in words and sentences
- Name words that start with the same sound

Phonemic Awareness (Isolation)
- Identify the first sound in a spoken word
- Identify the ending sound in a spoken word

Alphabet Knowledge
- Tell the difference between letters, pictures, and other symbols
- Recognize and name letters in own first and last name
- Position capitals right-side up
- Point to and name capital letters
- Position lowercase letters right-side up
- Point to and name lowercase letters
- Match all capital and lowercase letters

Concepts About Print
- Distinguish print from pictures
- Understand that print can be read and has meaning
- Find print in the classroom
- Hold book right-side up
- Open book at title page
- Point to front cover, back cover, pages, and spine
- Point to the title, author, and illustrator of a book
- Say what titles, authors, and illustrators do
- Imitate reading behaviors when handling books
- Turn pages from front to back, one at a time
- Follow print from top to bottom, left to right on a page
- Point to print moving left to right; sweep to next line, starting at left
- Tell the difference between a written sentence, word, and letter
- Recognize own name in print
- Recognize the names of friends and family in print
- Recognize important signs in our world

Comprehension

- Listen for enjoyment
- Listen to gain and share information
- Listen to perform a task
- Listen to learn what happened in a story
- Listen to converse with an adult or peer
- Choose a favorite book
- Identify favorite part of story
- Enjoy books and reading activities
- Demonstrate interest in read aloud time
- Make a prediction about a book by looking at pictures/illustrations
- Use prior knowledge to make predictions about a story
- Identify the beginning, middle, and end of a story
- Order the events of a story correctly using pictures
- Identify the main character in a story
- Identify where a story takes place
- Describe the problem/solution of a story
- Identify and name emotions in a story
- Identify parts of a story that are real and not real
- Explain how a story connects to personal experience
- Describe connections between stories
- Retell a story or event with pictures
- Re-enact a story or event
- Listen to stories, plays, and poems and talk about their meaning
- Generate a list of facts from an informational text
- Describe a topic after listening to an informational text
- Participate in a discussion restating facts about the topic of an informational text
- Learn about a topic and relate it to real life
- Categorize topics from informational texts by commonality
- Make comparisons based on information in informational texts

Oral Language

- Repeat teacher's words
- Demonstrate active listening by attending to stories and instruction
- Learn words linked to content being taught
- Use new words linked to content being taught
- Ask and respond to simple questions: Who? What? When? Where?
- Listen to follow directions (up to 3-4 steps)
- Complete a task by following oral directions (up to 3 steps)
- Use manners in conversation
- Speak with normal, conversational volume, tone, and inflection
- Communicate thoughts with words
- Communicate feelings with words
- Share opinions and ideas in conversation and discussion
- Talk about experiences and observations
- Speak in complete sentences made up of three or more words
- Use words to describe an object or a person's traits
- Use correct sentence formation
- Listen to sentences to judge if they "make sense"
- Describe everyday routines and events
- Tell stories

Writing

- Enjoy writing and engage in writing activities individually or with a group
- Share drawings and writing with others
- Watch teacher write sentences and read them aloud (up to 3)
- Recognize that stories can be documented in print, pictures, play, or through dictation/LEA
- Participate in Language Experiences (LEA) to retell classroom events and stories
- Dictate labels for objects, pictures, and objects in pictures
- Write scribbles, letter-like forms, or actual letters to represent words and ideas
- Hold a crayon with proper grip to write
- Use helping hand to stabilize objects and papers
- Trace capital letters
- Choose topics and generate ideas about which to write
- Understand there is a way to write that conveys meaning

Social-Emotional Benchmarks

Children in Pre-K have a wide variety of skills. Some may have exceptional motor skills, while others may excel in socialization. Children need practice in all areas of development, which is why many of our activities—although specific to fostering early math, literacy, and writing skills—have social and motor components.

Social-Emotional

We believe that some of the best ways to develop social-emotional wellness in children is to nurture:

- Innovation
- Responsibility
- Teamwork
- Perseverance
- Independence

Today, we have many young English language learners who need reassurance that they are safe and accepted. Depending on their culture, there may be things you notice about the ways children socially engage with their peers. It's important for Pre-K teachers to understand that English language learners may misinterpret gestures and social interactions. For example in some cultures, children may look down when speaking to an adult as a sign of respect. Regardless of their understanding of and ability to speak English, all four-year-olds need guidance and support in building strong social and emotional skills.

What are we teaching?

Our activities are designed to develop self-concept, self-regulation, personal initiative, emotional understanding, and relationships with adults and peers. We want children to have positive self esteem, engage in classroom activities, transition appropriately, take initiative, understand feelings, and take turns sharing and playing with their friends.

How do we do it?

- Model ways to show respect for self, people, things.
- Recognize, name, and respond to feelings. I can tell you are _____ because you are _____.
- Set class rules and teach children to follow them.
- Read stories that introduce children to values. The "Three Little Pigs" teach hard work and hard bricks save the day (visit Book Connection in this teacher's guide).
- Teach children how to help each other, for example, work together to lift and carry, to sweep into a dustpan, to say "stop" when someone is hurting, to sit beside a sad friend, and so forth.
- Participate in song, take turns, and share.

Social-Emotional Benchmarks

Self-Concept

- Demonstrate positive self esteem
- Demonstrate self-care skills like using the bathroom and dressing (putting on coats, washing hands) as age-/ability-appropriate
- Name body parts
- Describe changes in own body
- Imitate teacher's body movements

Self-Regulation

- Separate from caregiver without stress
- Manage emotions through negotiation and cooperation
- Respond to difficulty without harming self or others
- Manage and handle transitions well and without incident
- Understand and follow classroom routines
- Participate in clean up routines with other children
- Treat property with respect

Personal Initiative

- Demonstrate a desire for independence
- Show interest in many different activities

Emotional Understanding

- Name feelings he or she is experiencing
- Name emotions displayed by others
- Show empathy to others by offering comfort and help when appropriate

Relationships with Adults

- Interact easily with familiar adults
- Ask for help when needed
- Participate in conflict resolution activities (e.g., puppets acting out scenarios)

Relationships with Peers

- Cooperate with other children
- Participate in imaginary and dramatic play
- Take turns with peers
- Work with others to solve problems

Sensory Motor Benchmarks

Children will naturally engage in discovery and exploration. All you need to do is make materials accessible to interact freely. Some of the best ways to develop sensory motor skills is to engage in activities that promote:

- Movement
- Building and sorting
- Manipulation
- Processing sensations
- Organization

Our activities are hands-on, so children will experience sensory motor learning seamlessly in all that they do. As with social-emotional skills, some children will be better at sensory motor skills than others. In literacy we use finger plays, sing, dance, make actions, color, and trace letters. You will notice our manipulatives have unique features to encourage motor development. For example, children use their index fingers to trace letters with A-B-C Touch & Flip® Cards, and they move cards to position them for use.

What are we teaching?
Our literacy and math activities encourage handedness, fine and gross motor movements, correct crayon grip, tool use, manipulation, motor coordination, motor planning, and body awareness.

How do we do it?
- Use music that encourages movement, finger plays, counting with fingers, clapping, and tapping.
- Set out manipulatives or selected pieces (Sound Around Box™, A-B-C Touch & Flip Cards) and allow children to discover and explore freely.
- Allow children to hold books, turn pages, and point to letters and pictures.
- Use counters, blocks, and other items that can be counted, stacked, and sorted.
- Model proper tool use and manipulation—children may not always understand ways to manipulate pieces.
- Promote coloring and tracing of letters and numbers.

Sensory Motor Benchmarks

Fine Motor
- Use same hand consistently for holding crayons, toothbrush, utensils, and for performing skilled tasks
- Use fingers to open and close fasteners, hold crayons, scissors, cards, beads, etc.
- Move an object in one hand to position it for use, placement, or release
- Use index finger to trace letters or numbers on cards or in the air
- Move fingers to show age/number and for finger plays

Gross Motor
- Use large muscle groups to maintain posture/position and mobility (e.g., walk, run, hop, skip, jump, climb stairs)

Bilateral Motor Coordination
- Use helping hand to stabilize objects and papers
- Use both sides of the body in activities (e.g., using drumsticks, playing other instruments, dancing)

Visual Motor Control
- Look at hands and use visual cues to guide reaching for, grasping, and moving objects

Body Awareness
- Know where the body is in relation to space
- Use the right amount of pressure when holding and using tools
- Reach across midline to get an object from other side

Movement Perception
- Tolerate motion in activities
- Play with body awareness, balance, and regard for people and equipment

Touch Perception
- Handle play and art materials without an avoidance response
- Perceive the size, shape, or identity of an object by sense of touch

Visual Perception
- Notice and attach meaning to visual information

Motor Planning
- Move naturally and place body to perform tasks

School to Home Connection

Research consistently shows that a strong school to home connection helps children build self esteem, curiosity, and motivation to learn new things. Home and school are the two most important places to young children. A successful teacher/family partnership assures children that there are people who care about them. Both families and teachers can provide a unique perspective about the child, so open, regular, and meaningful communication is important.

When teachers and parents team up, everyone wins!

Here are 10 ways to make a strong school to home connection:

1. Find opportunities to communicate during planned preschool events like teacher/family meetings, conferences, and school visits. Take a few extra steps to communicate through letters, email, and even podcasts.

2. Share important assessment information about a child. Most schools have regular family reports to share key progress details. Use our Get Set for School® Pre-K readiness assessments to help you identify what your children know and can do, and easily share information with families and other educators. You can find them at **getsetforschool.com**

3. Share your curriculum with families. Show caregivers this Get Set for School Language & Literacy program. Let them play with some of the products. Tell them about our website, getsetforschool.com, so that they can explore the many resources there.

4. Share music with families. Send them home singing songs from our *Get Set for School Sing Along* CD or our new *Sing, Sound & Count With Me* CD. If there is a fun song that families sing at home, ask them to share it with you.

5. Reinforce learning at home. Encourage families to do finger plays and read books and nursery rhymes at home. Let them know just how important it is to their child's growth and development. Consider a teacher/family sharing day where family members can learn some of the finger plays and reading strategies for children. For families whose children's first language is not English, encourage them to sing songs and rhymes in their home language.

6. Model language and thinking skills out loud. Children benefit from hearing adults talk and solve problems. They learn vocabulary and critical thinking skills. Families can share thoughts throughout the day. **It looks like it's going to rain outside. I'd better take an umbrella.**

7. Read, read, read! Reading to children is fun and it helps build comprehension and language skills. Families, read to your children regularly. It's perfectly fine for them to read books over and over to build memory and deepen comprehension.

8. Share *My Book* with families. Send it home when children have completed it. Encourage caregivers to read it with their child and share it with other family members.

9. Write, write, write! Help families prepare their children to write. Encourage them to learn proper grip and support their child in holding a crayon correctly. Children love to see their names in print. Help them write their names in block capitals. These are the first and easiest letters to write.

10. Help children recognize letters and notice that print is all around them. Point out signs, logos, and letters where ever you go.

Dear Family Member,

This year we are using the Get Set for School® Language & Literacy program in our classroom. Get Set for School is an engaging curriculum that prepares your children for kindergarten. It was created by educators who understand young children and know the skills needed for later school success.

Music is essential to Get Set for School. The program uses music and movement to excite and engage children. Children love singing songs about letters, rhymes, numbers, shapes, and more with the *Sing, Sound & Count With Me* CD recorded with Children's Music GRAMMY®-award winners, Cathy Fink and Marcy Marxer. The Get Set for School program also includes hands-on products that keep children involved in their learning and teaches specific skills.

Throughout the school year, your child may be asked to bring items from home to support classroom learning. Periodically, materials will also be sent home. For example, children will create their own personal storybooks, which will be sent home for you to read with your child.

If you would like additional information about Get Set for School, visit the website at getsetforschool.com. There are also resources there that you can download for practice and enjoyment at home.

Sincerely,

Date _____

Dear Family Member,

In our Get Set for School® Language & Literacy program, we are currently learning about

_____.

We are using _____ to help us learn.

Please help your child choose a/an _____ to bring to school on

_____ for this activity.

Sincerely,

Books, Books, Books

Books – An Inspiring Adventure

Books are an important part of a child's life and should be introduced as early as possible. Books open a child's life to a world of adventure. Nursery rhymes and fairy tales present excellent opportunities for children to begin their own journey. As they read stories, children get to explore new places, discover new ideas, and learn about new and exciting characters. Early exposure to these stories sparks their imagination, increases their vocabulary, and ignites a lifelong joy of reading and learning. Books encourage children to be inquisitive, forward thinkers and provide an amazing gift of knowledge.

By reading to young children, we inspire them to learn to read and continue reading as they get older. Books should be read with enthusiasm and plenty of expression. Children love to be read to and enjoy interactive reading. Children love to point out items on a page, predict what will happen, repeat a rhyme, or even act out part of a story.

Fostering the Love of Reading

Parents can promote their child's love of reading simply by reading to their children at home. A love of reading can also come through building a home library, giving books as a gift/reward, and obtaining a membership card to a local library. A more creative way of fostering reading is to help children create their own books or tell/act out their own stories. When it's storytime, let them pick a book. Parents should also ensure that children see them reading.

Read to children continuously. You can serve as a model for parents who struggle with reading. Children will get into books with a teacher who makes characters come alive and makes reading books a grand adventure. The use of entertaining voices, sound effects, gestures, and expression can make children love storytime and books.

Selecting Books

Selecting books for children can be a difficult task. First, it is good to understand the types of books that are available for a specific age range. Next, it is important to discover the types of books a child likes. Allowing children to browse books at the library and bookstore can help with selection. Websites, teachers, librarians, and other parents are also good sources for book recommendations. After choosing a book, browse and assess it to determine if it's appropriate for your audience. Choosing the right book is an excellent start to a child's lifelong reading adventure. We have provided several options in the Book Connection section on pages 180–183.

When selecting books for Pre-K children:
- Tap into children's natural interests.
- Choose books that can be read in about five minutes.
- Emphasize repetitive and rhyming phrases.
- Select books that show diversity in culture, race, and gender.

Organizing Books

Books organized by subject make it easier for children to quickly find the books that interest them. Try placing similar subjects in bins around the room and label them with a picture and print (e.g., place a picture of a Triceratops on the bin with the word dinosaur). Also place props in the bins to entice children to re-enact the story using concrete objects. Encourage children to explore books and share their favorite books with their friends.

Encouraging Parents to Read

Many parents do not read regularly to their children. Your advice and encouragement can make all the difference for parents. Remind them that regularly reading books with their child will almost ensure that their child will love learning. Mem Fox, a literacy expert, has influenced and inspired our thinking on parents reading to children. Ms. Fox has published more than 30 books for children and taught literacy for more than 25 years. She believes that there is an important bond that develops as parent and child share in the joys and adventures of books. Ms. Fox also strongly emphasizes that reading aloud to children every day is key to their later success in school and life.

Beyond helping the reluctant parent readers, you will also need to work with parents who don't know how to read. In this situation, steer them to the librarians. Librarians know books and children and they know how to put them together. At storytimes, librarians read to children, modeling for parents how to read to children of different ages and stages.

Book Connection

We recommend reading related books to further expand the concepts in our *Language & Literacy Pre-K Teacher's Guide*. Each book on the list engages children with simple, inviting text and clear, attractive illustrations. The books are an appropriate length for Pre-K read-alouds. We hope you enjoy reading them as much as we did.

Phonological Awareness

Clara Caterpillar by Pamela Duncan Edwards. Illustrated by Henry Cole.
Catisha Caterpillar looks down on Clara Caterpillar because of her lack of color. The story, full of alliterative text, takes a turn when Catisha faces danger.

Cock-a-Doodle-Moo by Bernard Most.
What happens when a rooster loses his voice and can't deliver his cock-a-doodle-doo? His friend the cow steps in to help. Bright, bold illustrations with cartoon-like balloons deliver the animal sounds.

The Fat Cat Sat on the Mat by Nurit Karlan.
What happens when a fat cat sits on a rat's mat? Find out in fun, rhythmic text and repetitive sounds.

Favorite Nursery Rhymes from Mother Goose. Illustrated by Scott Gustafson.
Beautiful illustrations capture children's imagination as they read these classic rhymes.

Hello Baby by Mem Fox. Illustrated by Steve Jenkins.
Children will love learning about baby animals through this book's rhythmic text and cut-paper illustrations. A surprise ending reveals a human baby.

If You Were Alliteration (Word Fun) by Trisha Speed Shaskan. Illustrated by Sara Gray.
Striking colors engage children who ponder what they could do if they were an alliteration.

Is Your Mama a Llama? by Deborah Guarino.
Lloyd the baby llama asks all of his animal friends if their mamas are also llamas. Children will love the rhyming riddles as the baby animals help Lloyd discover that not all animal mamas are llamas.

One Duck Stuck: A Mucky Ducky Counting Book by Phyllis Root. Illustrated by Jane Chapman.
Filled with giggle producing sound effects, this book follows the story of a duck that can't seem to get unstuck from the mud. The story is rich with color and teaches children to count to 10.

Playtime Rhymes for Little People by Clare Beaton.
Forty classic nursery rhymes are delivered with hand sewn illustrations that pop off of the page.

Polar Bear, Polar Bear, What Do You Hear? by Bill Martin Jr. Illustrated by Eric Carle.
Filled with colorful and lively illustrations, this book takes children to one of their favorite places, the zoo. Children will enjoy the rhythmic text and making the sounds of the zoo animals.

Rhyming Dust Bunnies by Jan Thomas.
Four dust bunny friends show off their abilities to rhyme words. Full of brilliant colors and a fun-loving, silly nature, young children will love learning to rhyme with this book.

Ten-Second Tongue Twisters by Mike Artell. Illustrated by Buck Jones.
Tongue twisters full of alliteration similar to "Peter Piper" will have children laughing.

Alphabet Knowledge

Chicka Chicka Boom Boom by Bill Martin Jr. & John Archambault. Illustrated by Lois Ehlert.
Racing letters and rhythmic text help children gleefully repeat the ABCs. Bold colors enliven the wild tale.

Dinosaur A-Z by Roger Priddy.
Dinosaur enthusiasts will love meeting a new dinosaur for each letter of the alphabet. Includes realistic dinosaur models and pronunciation guide.

Dr. Seuss's ABC: An Amazing Alphabet Book! by Dr. Seuss.
Children will love learning the alphabet with the book's rhythmic text and zany pictures.

Concepts About Print

Andy That's My Name by Tomiede Paola.
Big kids ignore Andy because they say he's too little. But they do use his name to make many words.

Chrysanthemum by Kevin Henkes.
Chrysanthemum always thought her name was special. The first day of school changes her opinion.

Mommy Doesn't Know My Name by Suzanne Williams. Illustrated by Andrew Shachat.
Hannah's mother constantly calls her by little pet names. She wonders if her mother knows her real name. Children will enjoy how Hannah imagines herself as the pet names her mother endearingly calls her.

Comprehension

Big Al by Andrew Clements.
Big Al can't make friends because of his size. Things change when the other fish are caught in a net.

Caps For Sale by Esphyr Slobodkina.
A cap peddler awakes to find all of his caps missing. Repetition and rhythm add to the entertaining story.

Corduroy by Don Freeman.
What really happens when a store closes for the night? Corduroy the teddy bear finds out as he searches for his missing button. Children will be full of wonder as they discover what happens to Corduroy.

An Extraordinary Egg by Leo Lionni.
Jessica the frog thinks her new friend is a chicken in this tale of friendship and mistaken identity.

Goldilocks and the Three Bears by Jan Brett.
This retelling captures the traditional story with intricate detail that children will enjoy time and time again.

Green Eggs and Ham by Dr. Seuss.
Pushy and eccentric Sam-I-Am tries to get an unknown character to eat green eggs and ham.

Guess How Much I Love You by Sam McBratney. Illustrated by Anita Jeram.
A father and son find exciting and creative ways to say how much they love each other.

The Hare and the Tortoise and other Fables of La Fontaine by Ranjit Bolt.
Illustrated by Giselle Potter.
Classic fables take on a new lilt with these lighthearted rhymes. Includes classics such as "The Town Mouse and the Country Mouse" and "The Crow and the Fox."

Harriet, You'll Drive Me Wild by Mem Fox. Illustrated by Marla Frazee.
What does Harriet's mother do when Harriet continues to misbehave? Mem Fox beautifully captures the relationship of a mischievous daughter and frustrated mother. The realistic illustrations give life to the story.

If You Give a Mouse a Cookie by Laura Numeroff. Illustrated by Felicia Bond.
A young boy gives a mouse a cookie. What happens next is funny and sure to cause a giggle.

If You Hopped Like a Frog by David Schwartz. Illustrated by James Warhola.
Colorful illustrations and a beautifully crafted story help children see life as a frog or another animal.

Knuffle Bunny: A Cautionary Tale by Mo Willems.
This brilliantly narrated story follows Trixie and her dad to the laundromat. Upon their arrival home, she realizes she has a problem. Children will empathize with Trixie as she tries to solve her problem.

It's Mine! by Leo Lionni.
Milton, Rupert and Lydia are three frogs who spend their day bickering instead of sharing. After disaster strikes and they are saved by a toad, they learn the importance of getting along and sharing.

The Mitten by Jan Brett.
Nicki loses one of the mittens that his grandmother made. It is hard to find in the snow. One by one, several animals take cover in Nicki's mitten. Amazing colors and expression bring the animals to life.

My Big Dinosaur Book by Roger Priddy.
Who is a hungry hunter? Which dinosaur has two horns on its head? Check out the models of familiar dinosaurs and new friends to search for the answers.

Rainbow Fish by Marcus Pfister.
The Rainbow Fish is only concerned with his scales and their beauty and doesn't have any friends. He discovers the real value of friendship and beauty after seeking counsel from a wise octopus.

The Runaway Bunny by Margaret Wise.
When a little bunny runs away, the bunny's mother does not give up searching to bring the little one back home. The little bunny encounters several imaginary twists on the journey.

The Snowy Day by Ezra Jack Keats.
A little boy explores a city newly covered by snow. Watercolors and collage capture the snowy landscape.

Sleepy Bears by Mem Fox. Illustrated by Kerry Argent.
Children will identify with the cubs and their desire to stay up past bedtime, while Mother Bear knows exactly what to do. The book is full of rhymes and vivid colors.

Stellaluna by Janell Cannon.
Vivid illustrations illuminate a beautiful tale of a bat that survives an owl attack and is adopted by a bird.

The Three Little Pigs retold by Patricia Seibert. Illustrated by Horacia Elena.
The classic fairy tale about three little pigs. Whose home will survive the big bad wolf?

We're Going on a Bear Hunt by Michelle Vanston.
A family takes an amazing journey searching for a bear. They see many interesting places along the way.

What Do You Do With a Tail Like This? by Steve Jenkins and Robin Page.
What do you do with a tail like that? Children will be asked a question about different animal body parts. They can predict what will happen and will enjoy discovering the answer.

Oral Language

Brown Bear, Brown Bear, What Do You See? by Eric Carle.
This fun and easy pattern story encourages children to predict rhyming words. This is an excellent resource with bold and unique illustrations that teach descriptive language.

The Chocolate-Covered-Cookie Tantrum by Deborah Blumenthal.
This is a story of a classic temper tantrum. When Sophie does not get a cookie that she has asked for, she responds accordingly. Colorful and exaggerated illustrations truly capture the tantrum.

The Grouchy Ladybug by Eric Carle.
This engaging book shows the changing mood of an irritable bug that eventually adopts nicer behavior.

I Call My Hand Gentle by Amanda Haan.
This vividly colorful book teaches children about kindness and cooperation. It is beautifully illustrated with abstract artwork that children will love.

I Was So Mad by Mercer Mayer.
Little Critter gets really mad when his family won't let him do the things he wants to do. Young children will identify with Little Critter. This is a good book to get children to talk about feeling mad.

Please and Thank You Book by Richard Scarry.
Children will enjoy the animal characters as they are reminded to say "please" and "thank you." This is a fun book that also offers lessons on right and wrong.

Time to Say "Please"! by Mo Willems.
This fun book helps children understand how to be polite in certain situations. Young children and a group of mice teach these valuable lessons on manners.

Top Cat by Lois Ehlert.
A new kitten arrives, but not everyone is happy to see the newcomer. The older cat resists until he realizes the kitten is there to stay. Colorful, textured paper designs bring this story to life.

What Do You Say, Dear? by Sesyle Joslin. Illustrated by Maurice Sendak.
Unusual situations prompt children to show their manners. They will enjoy the silly illustrations and circumstances presented in this book.

Social-Emotional

A Cat and a Dog by Claire Masurel and Bob Kolar.
A cat and a dog live together and always fight. They find out that they can help each other.

From Head to Toe by Eric Carle.
This vividly colored book will have children up and moving. It helps them identify different body parts as they move around the room.

Giraffes Can't Dance by Giles Andreae. Illustrated by Guy Parker-Rees.
Friends tease Gerald the giraffe because he can't dance. With encouragement, he finds his own beat.

Hey Little Ant by Phillip and Hannah Hoose. Illustrated by Debbie Tilley.
A little boy's conversation with an ant teaches children about understanding and compassion. Children will enjoy the colorful and cartoon-like images.

Assessment

Families always want to know how their child is doing. Assessment helps you track what students know and can do. It allows you to share information about a child's learning with families, specialists, educators, and administrators.

Assessment can help you make good decisions for your children. Each assessment is a snapshot in time. Those snapshots over weeks and months show the path of a child's development and learning. This is the foundation for planning a curriculum—the set of experiences, activities, and materials you carefully select to help children learn.

We also assess young children to determine who would benefit from special services. Early identification helps families and schools address learning needs quickly.

Use Check for Understanding

Each activity in this teacher's guide focuses on a learning benchmark or skill. The Check for Understanding section helps you determine how well children understand or use the skill. We don't expect that your children will master each skill in one exposure. Young children need multiple opportunities to practice something before they really understand it. Use Check for Understanding to find out what your children understand so you can plan future experiences.

How We Check

In *Basics of Assessment: A Primer for Early Childhood Educators* (by McAfee, Leong, and Bodrova), the authors describe several ways to gather information about children. We use three of their methods in Check for Understanding.

Observe: Watch children as they move through an activity. What do they say? How do they move? What do they try? How do they solve problems? Collect this information so you can change course during the activity and make good decisions about future lessons.

> Sophie goes to the classroom library during choice time. She picks up a book and holds it right-side up. She starts turning pages from back to front. Her teacher notices and decides to work on directionality with Sophie.

Review Work Products: Children create drawings, constructions, graphs, dramatizations, and more on a daily basis. Review children's work to find evidence of what they know and can do.

> Wen and Madison want to make birthday cards for the class pet, a lizard. Madison gets frustrated because she cannot draw herself holding the lizard. Her teacher builds Mat Man with both children and models drawing a person. Wen and Madison make new cards. The teacher photocopies the before and after drawings done by both children for their portfolios.

Elicit Responses from Children: Responses can be answers to questions, parts of a discussion, participation in a task, and following directions. In children's responses, you can find clues to how they are thinking and what they understand.

At the end of The Print Gallery activity, Isaac's teacher asks him to pick a card. Isaac correctly says that there is a word on the card. He picks another card and correctly says that it is a picture. His teacher knows that he understands the difference between pictures and words.

You can keep a record of children's learning using each of these assessment methods. Write an observation on a sticky note, photograph a child's creation in the block area, and write children's responses to a group discussion. These records help assess a child's progress over time. They also help share information with parents and other educators.

Kindergarten Readiness

We have developed a Literacy Assessment, available online at getsetforschool.com/click which allows you to easily see which benchmarks your children have mastered. We include an assessment for general kindergarten readiness in our *My First School Book* activity book. It covers many of the important skills that children need to know for success in kindergarten. Children name pictures, colors, letters, and numbers. They also copy shapes, draw a person, and write their names. Send a copy of the completed assessment home with families at the end of the year.

Language & Literacy Pre-K Teaching Guidelines

Week	Monday	Tuesday	Wednesday
1	**Phonological Awareness** Identify the Sound "Do You Hear What I Hear?" pp. 30–31	**Alphabet Knowledge** Distinguish Letters from Pictures "Fishing for Letters" pp. 66–67	**Phonological Awareness** Identify the Sound "Guess the Sound" p. 31
	Oral Language Ask & Respond to Questions "Ask & Tell" pp. 134–135	**Concepts About Print** Distinguish Print from Pictures "Pictures and Words" pp. 90–91	**Oral Language** Use Manners "Manners in Action" pp. 144–145
2	**Phonological Awareness** Discriminate Sounds "Sound Detectives" pp. 32–33	**Alphabet Knowledge** Recognize Letters "Sing & Point with Me" pp. 68–69	**Phonological Awareness** Discriminate Sounds "Loud and Quiet" p. 33
	Oral Language Ask & Respond to Questions "All About Me" p. 135	**Concepts About Print** Recognize Book Parts "Book Parts" pp. 92–93	**Comprehension** Make Predictions "What Will Happen?" pp. 106–107
3	**Phonological Awareness** Discriminate Words "Same and Different Words" pp. 34–35	**Capital F – Alphabet Knowledge** Position Letters "Smiley Face Helper" p. 71	**Phonological Awareness** Discriminate Words "Color Words" p. 35
	Oral Language Ask & Respond to Questions "Who Am I?" p. 135	**Alphabet Knowledge** Recognize Letters in Name "Please Pass L" pp. 72–73	**Comprehension** Make Predictions "Pumpkin Life" p. 107
4	**Phonological Awareness** Recognize Rhyming Words "Rhyme Time" pp. 36–37	**Capital H – Alphabet Knowledge** Identify Capital Letters "Letter Time" pp. 78–79	**Phonological Awareness** Recognize Rhyming Words "Rhyming Animals" p. 37
	Oral Language Follow Directions "Follow Me" pp. 136–137	**Concepts About Print** Distinguish Print from Pictures "Picture Search" p. 91	**Comprehension** Make Predictions "It's in the Name" p. 107
5	**Phonological Awareness** Make Rhyming Words "I Know Words That Rhyme" pp. 38–39	**Capital I – Alphabet Knowledge** Identify Capital Letters "Capital Letter Sort" p. 79	**Phonological Awareness** Make Rhyming Words "Nursery Rhyme Mix" p. 39
	Oral Language Talk About Feelings "How Does It Feel?" pp. 138–139	**Concepts About Print** Recognize Book Parts "Book Show and Tell" p. 93	**Comprehension** Recognize Beginning, Middle & End "Beginning, Middle & End" pp. 108–109
6 **Review Week**	**Alphabet Knowledge** Review L, F, E, H, T, I, U Identify Capital Letters "Letter Hunt" p. 79	**Alphabet Knowledge** Distinguish Letters from Pictures "Signs All Around" p. 67	**Alphabet Knowledge** Review L, F, E, H, T, I, U Identify Capital Letters "Letter Hunt" p. 79
	Phonological Awareness Make Rhyming Words Discovery Teaching "Tickledee-dee" p. 29	**Oral Language** Follow Directions "Directions to the Treasure" p. 137	**Comprehension** Recognize Beginning, Middle & End "Ballet Dancing Truck Driver" p. 109
7	**Phonological Awareness** Find Words in a Sentence "Let's Break Sentences" pp. 40–41	**Capital C – Alphabet Knowledge** Identify Capital Letters "Letter Time" pp. 78–79	**Phonological Awareness** Find Words in a Sentence "Look in a Book" p. 41
	Alphabet Knowledge Identify Letters in Name "That's My Letter" pp. 74–75	**Oral Language** Talk About Experiences "Reach and Tell" pp. 140–141	**Comprehension** Find Main Character "Who Could It Be?" pp. 110–111
8	**Phonological Awareness** Build Sentences with Words "Let's Make Sentences" pp. 42–43	**Capital O – Alphabet Knowledge** Identify Letters in Name "Roll a Letter" p. 75	**Phonological Awareness** Build Sentences with Words "Tortoise and the Hare Sentences" p. 43
	Oral Language Learn New Words "What's the Word?" pp. 142–143	**Concepts About Print** Recognize Book Parts "Predict It" p. 93	**Comprehension** Find Main Character "Who's the Main One?" p. 111

Thursday	Friday	Notes
Alphabet Knowledge Distinguish Letters from Pictures "Sort Yourself" p. 67	**Phonological Awareness** Identify the Sound "Who Is It?" p. 31	
Concepts About Print Distinguish Print from Pictures "Pictures & Words" pp. 90–91	**Oral Language** Use Manners "Manners in Action" pp. 144–145	
Capital L – Alphabet Knowledge Position Letters "Letters Up!" pp. 70–71	**Phonological Awareness** Discriminate Sounds "It Doesn't Belong" p. 33	
Concepts About Print Recognize Book Parts "Book Parts" pp. 92–93	**Alphabet Knowledge** Recognize Letters "Silly Singing ABCs" p. 69	
Capital E – Alphabet Knowledge Position Letters "Are They Right?" p. 71	**Phonological Awareness** Discriminate Words "The Odd Word" p. 35	
Alphabet Knowledge Recognize Letters "Letter Leaders" p. 69	**Alphabet Knowledge** Recognize Letters in Name "Capital Call Out" p. 73	
Capital T – Alphabet Knowledge Identify Capital Letters "Letter Hunt" p. 79	**Phonological Awareness** Recognize Rhyming Words "I Can Find a Rhyme" p. 37	
Concepts About Print Distinguish Print from Pictures "Picture Search" p. 91	**Oral Language** Follow Directions "Follow the Dance" p. 137	
Capital U – Alphabet Knowledge Identify Capital Letters Discovery Teaching "Alphabet Cereal" p. 63	**Phonological Awareness** Make Rhyming Words "Silly Poem" p. 39	
Concepts About Print Recognize Book Parts "Book Show and Tell" p. 93	**Comprehension** Recognize Beginning, Middle & End "Draw & Act It Out" p. 109	
Phonological Awareness Recognize Rhyming Words Discovery Teaching "Books of Rhymes" p. 29	**Alphabet Knowledge** Review L, F, E, H, T, I, U Identify Capital Letters "Letter Hunt" p. 79	
Oral Language Talk About Feelings "Feelings Talk" p. 139	**Oral Language** Talk About Feelings "Book of Emotions" p. 139	
Alphabet Knowledge Recognize Letters in Name "Sing and Pop" p. 73	**Phonological Awareness** Find Words in a Sentence "I Can Count Words" p. 41	
Oral Language Talk About Experiences "School Trip" p. 141	**Comprehension** Find Main Character "More Adventures Ahead" p. 111	
Capital Q – Alphabet Knowledge Identify Capital Letters Discovery Teaching "Sensory Letters" p. 63	**Phonological Awareness** Build Sentences with Words "I Can Count My Words" p. 43	
Concepts About Print Recognize Book Parts "Predict It" p. 93	**Oral Language** Talk About Experiences "What's Your Experience?" p. 141	

Language & Literacy Pre-K Teaching Guidelines

Week	Monday	Tuesday	Wednesday
9	**Phonological Awareness** Find Words in a Sentence Discovery Teaching "Sentence Colors" p. 29	**Capital G – Alphabet Knowledge** Identify Capital Letters Discovery Teaching "Alphabet Cereal" p. 63	**Writing** Represent Events in a Story "Replay Robins" pp. 154–155
	Oral Language Learn New Words "Vocabulary Fishing" p. 143	**Concepts About Print** Follow Text Left to Right "Which Way Do We Go?" pp. 94–95	**Comprehension** Name the Place "What Can You See?" pp. 112–113
10	**Phonological Awareness** Make One Word into Two "Word Magic" pp. 44–45	**Capital J – Alphabet Knowledge** Identify Capital Letters Discovery Teaching "Roll-A-Dough Letters®" p. 63	**Phonological Awareness** Make One Word into Two "Picture That" p. 45
	Oral Language Learn New Words "What Am I?" p. 143	**Writing** Retell Through Play "Hat Play" pp. 156–157	**Comprehension** Name the Place "Where Could It Be?" p. 113
11	**Phonological Awareness** Make Two Words into One "Two Words, New Word" pp. 46–47	**Capital P – Alphabet Knowledge** Identify Capital Letters Discovery Teaching "Capitals with Letter Cards and Wood Pieces" p. 63	**Phonological Awareness** Make Two Words into One "Crazy Compound Words" p. 47
	Oral Language Learn New Words Discovery Teaching "Make the Most of Read-Alouds" p. 133	**Concepts About Print** Follow Text Left to Right "All Kinds of Pages" p. 95	**Comprehension** Describe Problem and Solution "What Should I Do?" pp. 114–115
12 Review Week	**Alphabet Knowledge** Review C, O, Q, G, S, J, D, P, B Identify Capital Letters Discovery Teaching "Letter Path" p. 63	**Oral Language** Learn New Words Discovery Teaching "Class Word Book" p. 133	**Alphabet Knowledge** Review C, O, Q, G, S, J, D, P, B Identify Capital Letters Discovery Teaching "Letter Path" p. 63
	Phonological Awareness Make Two Words into One "Give Me a Break" p. 45	**Concepts About Print** Follow Text Left to Right "Follow the Words" p. 95	**Comprehension** Describe Problem & Solution "Solution Twist'" p. 115
13	**Phonological Awareness** Recognize Syllables "Clap Names" pp. 48–49	**Capital R – Alphabet Knowledge** Identify Capital Letters "Letter Time" pp. 78–79	**Phonological Awareness** Recognize Syllables "Syllable Sort" p. 49
	Oral Language Learn New Words Discovery Teaching "Stretch It" p. 133	**Concepts About Print** Distinguish Print from Pictures "Words Tell a Story" p. 91	**Comprehension** Identify Emotions in a Story "Feelings Are Important" pp. 116–117
14	**Phonological Awareness** Recognize Syllables Discovery Teaching "Choose and Clap" p. 29	**Capital A – Alphabet Knowledge** Identify Capital Letters Discovery Teaching "Capitals with Letter Cards and Wood Pieces" p. 63	**Writing** Label Objects "Label the Teacher" pp. 160–161
	Oral Language Learn New Words "What's the Word?" pp. 142–143	**Concepts About Print** Distinguish Letters, Words & Sentences "Letters & Words for Sentences" pp. 96–97	**Comprehension** Identify Emotions in a Story "How Would You Feel?" p. 117
15	**Phonological Awareness** Divide Onset & Rime "Words Have Families Too" pp. 50–51	**Capital M – Alphabet Knowledge** Identify Capital Letters "Letter Hunt" p. 79	**Phonological Awareness** Divide Onset & Rime "Family Ties" p. 51
	Oral Language Learn New Words "Vocabulary Fishing" p. 143	**Concepts About Print** Distinguish Letters, Words & Sentences "Words and Letters in Our Room" p. 97	**Comprehension** Identify Emotions in a Story "Finding Feelings" p. 117
16	**Phonological Awareness** Combine Onset & Rime "I Say, You Say, We Say" pp. 52–53	**Capital W – Alphabet Knowledge** Identify Capital Letters Discovery Teaching "Sensory Letters" p. 63	**Phonological Awareness** Combine Onset & Rime "Matching Rimes" p. 53
	Oral Language Learn New Words "What Am I?" p. 143	**Concepts About Print** Distinguish Letters, Words & Sentences "Sentences About Me" p. 97	**Comprehension** Find Facts "Listening for Information" pp. 126–127

Thursday	Friday
Capital S – Alphabet Knowledge Identify Capital Letters Discovery Teaching "Capitals with Letter Cards and Wood Pieces" p. 63	**Writing** Represent Events in a Story "Add A Character" p. 155
Concepts About Print Follow Text Left to Right "Which Way Do We Go?" pp. 94–95	**Comprehension** Name the Place "Set the Stage" p. 113
Capital D – Alphabet Knowledge Identify Capital Letters Discovery Teaching "Slate Letters" p. 63	**Phonological Awareness** Make One Word into Two "Give Me a Break" p. 45
Writing Retell Through Play "Create a Prop" p. 157	**Writing** Represent Events in a Story "Character Change" p. 155
Capital B – Alphabet Knowledge Identify Capital Letters "Letter Hunt" p. 79	**Phonological Awareness** Make Two Words into One "I'll Give You Half" p. 47
Concepts About Print Follow Text Left to Right "All Kinds of Pages" p. 95	**Comprehension** Describe Problem and Solution "What Could They Do?" p. 115
Writing Retell Through Play "Isabel's Birthday" p. 157	**Alphabet Knowledge** Review C, O, Q, G, S, J, D, P, B Identify Capital Letters Discovery Teaching "Letter Path" p. 63
Concepts About Print Follow Text Left to Right "Follow the Words" p. 95	**Oral Language** Use Manners "Manners Relay" p. 145
Capital K – Alphabet Knowledge Identify Capital Letters Discovery Teaching "Alphabet Cereal" p. 63	**Phonological Awareness** Recognize Syllables "Syllable Compare" p. 49
Concepts About Print Distinguish Print from Pictures "Words Tell a Story" p. 91	**Writing** Dictate Information "Class Journal" pp. 158–159
Capital V – Alphabet Knowledge Identify Capital Letters Discovery Teaching "Roll-A-Dough Letters®" p. 63	**Writing** Label Objects "Room Label Rhyme" p. 161
Concepts About Print Distinguish Letters, Words & Sentences "Letters & Words for Sentences" pp. 96–97	**Writing** Dictate Information "Our Classroom Trip" p. 159
Capital N – Alphabet Knowledge Identify Capital Letters Discovery Teaching "Slate Letters" p. 63	**Phonological Awareness** Divide Onset & Rime "United We Stand" p. 51
Concepts About Print Distinguish Letters, Words & Sentences "Words and Letters in Our Room" p. 97	**Writing** Dictate Information "Explore Writing" p. 159
Capital X – Alphabet Knowledge Recognize Capital Letters "Identify Capital Letters" pp. 78–79	**Phonological Awareness** Combine Onset & Rime "Match the End" p. 53
Concepts About Print Distinguish Letters, Words & Sentences "Sentences About Me" p. 97	**Writing** Dictate Information Discovery Teaching "That's My Favorite" p. 153

Notes

Language & Literacy Pre-K Teaching Guidelines

Week	Monday	Tuesday	Wednesday
17	**Phonological Awareness** Divide Onset & Rime "Family Ties" p. 51	**Capital Y – Alphabet Knowledge** Identify Capital Letters "Capital Letter Sort" p. 79	**Alphabet Knowledge** Identify Letters in Name "Letter Tags" pp. 76–77
	Oral Language Learn New Words Discovery Teaching "Act It Out" p. 133	**Concepts About Print** Recognize Names "I Know My Name & Your Name Too" pp. 98–99	**Comprehension** Distinguish Real From Make-Believe "Is It Real?" pp. 118–119
18 Review Week	**Alphabet Knowledge** Review R, K, A, V, M, N, W, X, Y, Z Identify Capital Letters Discovery Teaching "Sensory Letters" p. 63	**Oral Language** Learn New Words Discovery Teaching "Class Word Book" p. 133	**Alphabet Knowledge** Review R, K, A, V, M, N, W, X, Y, Z Identify Capital Letters Discovery Teaching "Sensory Letters" p. 63
	Phonological Awareness Discriminate Words Discovery Teaching "Simon Says" p. 29	**Concepts About Print** Recognize Names "Sticky Names" p. 99	**Comprehension** Find Facts "Our Own Book" p. 127
19	**Phonological Awareness** Recognize Rhyming Words Discovery Teaching "Books of Rhymes" p. 29	**Lowercase c – Alphabet Knowledge** Identify Lowercase Letters Discovery Teaching "Double Line Blackboard" p. 65	**Oral Language** Use Manners "A Special Thanks" p. 145
	Oral Language Learn New Words Discovery Teaching "Picture Displays" p. 133	**Concepts About Print** Recognize Signs "I Can Read Signs" pp. 100–101	**Comprehension** Distinguish Real From Make-Believe "Tell Your Own Tale" p. 119
20	**Phonological Awareness** Repeat Beginning Sounds "In the Beginning" pp. 54–55	**Lowercase o – Alphabet Knowledge** Identify Lowercase Letters Discovery Teaching "A Letter Book" p. 65	**Phonological Awareness** Repeat Beginning Sounds "Starting Sound Shuffle" p. 55
	Oral Language Learn New Words Discovery Teaching "Make the Most of Read-Alouds" p. 133	**Concepts About Print** Recognize Signs "Push and Pull" p. 101	**Comprehension** Distinguish Real From Make-Believe "Book Sort" p. 119
21	**Phonological Awareness** Identify Beginning Sound "How Does It Begin?" pp. 56–57	**Lowercase v – Alphabet Knowledge** Identify Lowercase Letters Discovery Teaching "Match and Reveal" p. 65	**Phonological Awareness** Identify Beginning Sound "The Real Deal" p. 57
	Oral Language Learn New Words Discovery Teaching "Stretch It" p. 133	**Concepts About Print** Recognize Signs "Cut and Color" p. 101	**Comprehension** Make Personal Connections "Just Like Me" pp. 120–121
22	**Phonological Awareness** Identify Beginning Sound Discovery Teaching "Searching for Sounds" p. 29	**Lowercase t – Alphabet Knowledge** Identify Lowercase Letters Discovery Teaching "It's In the Book" p. 65	**Phonological Awareness** Repeat Beginning Sounds "Starting Sound Shuffle" p. 55
	Oral Language Learn New Words "What's the Word?" pp. 142–143	**Writing** Share Ideas "Sign Makers" pp. 162–163	**Comprehension** Make Personal Connections "My Birthday Story" p. 121
23	**Phonological Awareness** Recognize Rhyming Words "Rhyme Time" pp. 36–37	**lowercase d – Alphabet Knowledge** Identify Lowercase Letters "Lowercase Limbo" pp. 80–81	**Phonological Awareness** Recognize Rhyming Words "Rhyming Animals" p. 37
	Oral Language Learn New Words "Vocabulary Fishing" p. 143	**Concepts About Print** Recognize Book Parts Discovery Teaching "Child's Choice" p. 89	**Comprehension** Make Connections Between Stories "What's Alike?" pp. 122–123
24 Review Week	**Alphabet Knowledge** Review c, o, s, v, w, t, a, d, g Identify Lowercase Letters "Lowercase Look & See" p. 81	**Oral Language** Learn New Words Discovery Teaching "Class Word Book" p. 133	**Alphabet Knowledge** Review c, o, s, v, w, t, a, d, g Identify Lowercase Letters "Lowercase Look & See" p. 81
	Phonological Awareness Make Two Words into One "I'll Give You Half" p. 47	**Concepts About Print** Recognize Names "Famous Faces" p. 99	**Comprehension** Make Connections Between Stories "Connections Match" p. 123

Thursday	Friday
Capital Z – Alphabet Knowledge Identify Capital Letters Discovery Teaching "Alphabet Cereal" p. 63	**Comprehension** Find Facts "We're the Experts" p. 127
Concepts About Print Recognize Names "I Know My Name & Your Name Too" pp. 98–99	**Writing** Dictate Information "Our Class Journal" pp. 158–159
Writing Label Objects "Explore Science" p. 161	**Alphabet Knowledge** Review R, K, A, V, M, N, W, X, Y, Z Identify Capital Letters Discovery Teaching "Sensory Letters" p. 63
Concepts About Print Recognize Names "Sticky Names" p. 99	**Writing** Dictate Information "Our Classroom Trip" p. 159
Alphabet Knowledge Identify Letters in Name "Last Names" p. 75	**Alphabet Knowledge** Identify Letters in Name "Names in Our Class" p. 77
Concepts About Print Recognize Signs "I Can Read Signs" pp. 100–101	**Writing** Dictate Information "Explore Writing" p. 159
Lowercase s – Alphabet Knowledge Identify Lowercase Letters Discovery Teaching "Letters in Names" p. 65	**Phonological Awareness** Repeat Beginning Sounds "Tongue Twister Twist" p. 55
Concepts About Print Recognize Signs "Push and Pull" p. 101	**Writing** Dictate Information Discovery Teaching "That's My Favorite" p. 153
Lowercase w – Alphabet Knowledge Match Capital & Lowercase Letters Discovery Teaching "Capital Partners" p. 65	**Phonological Awareness** Identify Beginning Sound "Look in a Book" p. 57
Concepts About Print Recognize Signs "Cut and Color" p. 101	**Writing** Dictate Information "Class Journal" pp. 158–159
Lowercase a – Alphabet Knowledge Identify Lowercase Letters Discovery Teaching "Letter Hunt" p. 65	**Comprehension** Make Personal Connections "More Stories Like Mine" p. 121
Writing Share Ideas "Stop and Go" p. 163	**Writing** Dictate Information "Our Classroom Trip" p. 159
Lowercase g – Alphabet Knowledge Identify Lowercase Letters "Lowercase Letter Laugh" p. 81	**Comprehension** Make Connections Between Stories "Tell a Connecting Story" p. 123
Concepts About Print Recognize Book Parts Discovery Teaching "Child's Choice" p. 89	**Writing** Dictate Information "Explore Writing" p. 159
Writing Share Ideas "Write and Play" p. 163	**Alphabet Knowledge** Review c, o, s, v, w, t, a, d, g Identify Lowercase Letters "Lowercase Look & See" p. 81
Concepts About Print Recognize Names "Famous Faces" p. 99	**Writing** Share Ideas Discovery Teaching "Color to Conversation" p. 153

Language & Literacy Pre-K Teaching Guidelines

Week	Monday	Tuesday	Wednesday
25	**Phonological Awareness** Recognize Syllables Discovery Teaching "I Am a Fine Musician" p. 29	**Lowercase u – Alphabet Knowledge** Identify Lowercase Letters Discovery Teaching "Match and Reveal" p. 65	**Phonological Awareness** Recognize Syllables Discovery Teaching "Choose and Clap" p. 29
	Oral Language Learn New Words "What Am I?" p. 143	**Oral Language** Use Words That Describe "Touch or Look" pp. 146–147	**Comprehension** Retell a Story "You Caught Me!" pp. 124–125
26	**Phonological Awareness** Identify Final Sound "The End" pp. 58–59	**Lowercase e – Alphabet Knowledge** Identify Lowercase Letters Discovery Teaching "I Spy" p. 65	**Phonological Awareness** Identify Final Sound "Sound Stretch" p. 59
	Oral Language Learn New Words Discovery Teaching "Act It Out" p. 133	**Oral Language** Use Words That Describe "Silly Sentences" p. 147	**Comprehension** Retell a Story "Retell and Re-enact" p. 125
27	**Phonological Awareness** Identify Final Sound "The End" pp. 58–59	**Lowercase k– Alphabet Knowledge** Identify Letters in Name Discovery Teaching "Letters in Names" p. 65	**Phonological Awareness** Identify Final Sound "Matching Sounds" p. 59
	Oral Language Learn New Words Discovery Teaching "Picture Displays" p. 133	**Concepts About Print** Recognize Book Parts Discovery Teaching "Child's Choice" p. 89	**Comprehension** Find Facts "Listening for Information" pp. 126–127
28	**Alphabet Knowledge** Identify Letters in Name Discovery Teaching "Sign In, Please" p. 63	**Lowercase j – Alphabet Knowledge** Identify Lowercase Letters "Lowercase Limbo" pp. 80–81	**Writing** Represent Events in a Story "Replay Robins" pp. 154–155
	Oral Language Learn New Words Discovery Teaching "Make the Most of Read-Alouds" p. 133	**Alphabet Knowledge** Match Capital & Lowercase Letters "Letter Friends" pp. 82–83	**Comprehension** Find Facts "We're the Experts" p. 127
29	**Phonological Awareness** Find Words in a Sentence Discovery Teaching "Sentence Colors" p. 29	**Lowercase r – Alphabet Knowledge** Identify Lowercase Letters Discovery Teaching "Letter Hunt" p. 65	**Writing** Represent Events in a Story "Character Change" p. 155
	Oral Language Learn New Words Discovery Teaching "Stretch It" p. 133	**Alphabet Knowledge** Identify Letters in Name "Sun Letters" p. 77	**Comprehension** Sort Information "We Belong Together" pp. 128–129
30 **Review Week**	**Alphabet Knowledge** Review u, i, e, l, k, y, j, p, r, n Identify Lowercase Letters "Lowercase Letter Laugh" p. 81	**Oral Language** Learn New Words Discovery Teaching "Class Word Book" p. 133	**Alphabet Knowledge** Review u, i, e, l, k, y, j, p, r, n Identify Lowercase Letters "Lowercase Letter Laugh" p. 81
	Phonological Awareness Make Two Words into One "I'll Give You Half" p. 47	**Alphabet Knowledge** Match Capital & Lowercase Letters "Letter Marks the Spot" p. 83	**Comprehension** Sort Information "Musical Instruments" p. 129
31	**Phonological Awareness** Recognize Syllables Discovery Teaching "Sing Your Name" p. 29	**Lowercase m – Alphabet Knowledge** Match Capital & Lowercase Letters "Capital and Lowercase Collage" p. 83	**Writing** Retell Through Play "Create a Prop" p. 157
	Oral Language Learn New Words "What's the Word?" pp. 142–143	**Oral Language** Tell a Story "Tell Me About It" pp. 148–149	**Comprehension** Make Predictions Discovery Teaching "Whys and What Ifs?" p. 105
32	**Phonological Awareness** Divide Onset & Rime "United We Stand" p. 51	**Lowercase h – Alphabet Knowledge** Identify Lowercase Letters Discovery Teaching "I Spy" p. 65	**Writing** Retell Through Play "Isabel's Birthday" p. 157
	Oral Language Learn New Words "Vocabulary Fishing" p. 143	**Oral Language** Tell a Story "The End?" p. 149	**Comprehension** Find Facts "Listening for Information" pp. 126–127

Thursday	Friday
Lowercase i – Alphabet Knowledge Identify Lowercase Letters Discovery Teaching "Double Line Blackboard" p. 65	**Comprehension** Retell a Story "Sing, Say, and Act" p. 125
Oral Language Use Words That Describe "Taste or Smell" p. 147	**Writing** Make a Topic Choice "Just Like You!" pp. 164–165
Lowercase l – Alphabet Knowledge Identify Lowercase Letters "Capital and Lowercase Collage" p. 83	**Phonological Awareness** Identify Final Sound "Matching Sounds" p. 59
Oral Language Use Words That Describe "Touch or Look" pp. 146–147	**Writing** Make a Topic Choice "I Choose You" p. 165
Lowercase y – Alphabet Knowledge Match Capital & Lowercase Letters "Match Makers" pp. 84–85	**Comprehension** Find Facts "Our Own Book" p. 127
Concepts About Print Recognize Book Parts Discovery Teaching "Child's Choice" p. 89	**Writing** Make a Topic Choice "Jobs in Our Community" p. 165
Lowercase p – Alphabet Knowledge Identify Lowercase Letters "Lowercase Look and See" p. 81	**Writing** Dictate Information "Class Journal" pp. 158–159
Alphabet Knowledge Match Capital & Lowercase Letters "Letter Marks the Spot" p. 83	**Writing** Represent Events in a Story "Add a Character" p. 155
Lowercase n – Alphabet Knowledge Identify Lowercase Letters Discovery Teaching "A Letter Book" p. 65	**Comprehension** Sort Information "They're Good for You" p. 129
Phonological Awareness Find Words in a Sentence "I Can Count Words" p. 41	**Writing** Dictate Information "Our Classroom Trip" p. 159
Writing Retell Through Play "Hat Play" pp. 156–157	**Alphabet Knowledge** Review u, i, e, l, k, y, j, p, r, n Identify Lowercase Letters "Lowercase Letter Laugh" p. 81
Phonological Awareness Make Two Words into One "Crazy Compound Words" p. 47	**Writing** Dictate Information "Explore Writing" p. 159
Alphabet Knowledge Identify Letters in Name "Last Names Too" p. 77	**Oral Language** Tell a Story "It Happens Every Day" p. 149
Phonological Awareness Recognize Syllables "Syllable Sound-Off" p. 27	**Writing** Dictate Information "Explore Writing" p. 159
Lowercase b – Alphabet Knowledge Identify Lowercase Letters Discovery Teaching "Match and Reveal" p. 65	**Alphabet Knowledge** Match Capital & Lowercase Letters "Challenging Match" p. 85
Phonological Awareness Distinguish Sounds Discovery Teaching "Apples and Bananas" p. 29	**Writing** Share Ideas Discovery Teaching "Color to Conversation" p. 153

Notes

Language & Literacy Pre-K Teaching Guidelines

Week	Monday	Tuesday	Wednesday
33	**Phonological Awareness** Combine Onset & Rime "I Say, You Say, We Say" pp. 52–53	**Lowercase f – Alphabet Knowledge** Identify Lowercase Letters Discovery Teaching "It's In the Book" p. 65	**Writing** Label Objects Discovery Teaching "Science Labels" p. 153
	Oral Language Learn New Words "What Am I?" p. 143	**Comprehension** Retell a Story "You Caught Me!" pp. 124–125	**Comprehension** Retell a Story Discovery Teaching "Go For Drama" p. 105
34	**Phonological Awareness** Repeat Beginning Sounds "Tongue Twister Twist" p. 55	**Lowercase x – Alphabet Knowledge** Identify Lowercase Letters Discovery Teaching "Double Line Blackboard" p. 65	**Comprehension** Sort Information "We Belong Together" pp. 128–129
	Oral Language Learn New Words Discovery Teaching "Act it Out" p. 133	**Concepts About Print** Recognize Names "Sticky Names" p. 99	**Writing** Label Objects "Explore Science" p. 161
35	**Alphabet Knowledge** Review m, h, b, f, q, x, z Identify Lowercase Letters "Lowercase Limbo" pp. 80–81	**Phonological Awareness** Identify Beginning Sound "How Does It Begin?" pp. 56–57	**Alphabet Knowledge** Review m, h, b, f, q, x, z Identify Lowercase Letters "Lowercase Limbo" pp. 80–81
	Oral Language Learn New Words Discovery Teaching "Picture Displays" p. 133	**Alphabet Knowledge** Match Capital & Lowercase Letters "Circle a Letter" p. 85	**Comprehension** Dictate Information Discovery Teaching "My Favorite Part" p. 105
36 **Review Week**	**Alphabet Knowledge** Match Capital & Lowercase Letters Discovery Teaching "Capital Partners" p. 65	**Oral Language** Learn New Words Discovery Teaching "Class Word Book" p. 133	**Alphabet Knowledge** Identify Capital Letters Discovery Teaching "Letter Path" p. 63
	Comprehension Make Personal Connections Discovery Teaching "After You're Done" p. 105	**Phonological Awareness** Identify Final Sound "Matching Sounds" p. 59	**Comprehension** Find Facts "We're the Experts" p. 127

Thursday	Friday	Notes
Lowercase q – Alphabet Knowledge Match Capital & Lowercase Letters "Letter Friends" pp. 82–83	**Alphabet Knowledge** Identify Letters in Name "Names in Our Class" p. 77	
Phonological Awareness Combine Onset & Rime "Matching Rimes" p. 53	**Writing** Make a Topic Choice "Just Like You!" pp. 164–165	
Lowercase z – Alphabet Knowledge Match Capital & Lowercase Letters "Match Makers" pp. 84–85	**Comprehension** Recognize Beginning, MIddle & End "Ballet Dancing Truck Driver" p. 109	
Concepts About Print Recognize Names "Sticky Names" p. 99	**Writing** Make a Topic Choice "I Choose You" p. 165	
Phonological Awareness Identify Beginning Sound "The Real Deal" p. 57	**Alphabet Knowledge** Review m, h, b, f, q, x, z Identify Lowercase Letters "Lowercase Limbo" pp. 80–81	
Writing Share Ideas "Sign Makers" pp. 162–163	**Writing** Make a Topic Choice "Jobs in Our Community" p. 165	
Writing Share Ideas "Write and Play" p. 163	**Alphabet Knowledge** Match Capital & Lowercase Letters "Letter Marks the Spot" p. 83	
Phonological Awareness Identify Final Sound "Sound Stretch" p. 59	**Writing** Share Ideas Discovery Teaching "Color to Conversation" p. 153	

Vocabulary Words for Children

A
action – something you do
alphabet – the letters of a language
audience – a group of people who listen to you talk
author – person who writes a story

B
back – opposite side of the front
beginning – the first part, the start of something

C
capital – a large letter
category – a group of things that have something in common
common – something that you see a lot
compare – to look at similarities and differences
compound word – a word made up of two smaller words

D
describe – to tell what you notice about a person or object
different – not the same

E
end – the last part of something
environment – the world around you
experience – what has happened or is happening to you

F
fact – a piece of true information
feelings – something we have when we are happy, sad, angry, mad, or excited
first – before everything else, at the beginning
front – the part of something that comes first

G
greeting – a way to say "hello" to someone

I
illustrator – person who colors or draws pictures for a story

L
last – after everything else, at the end
letter – written marks that are part of the alphabet
lowercase – a small letter

M

main character – person or object the story is mainly about
make-believe – not real, imaginary
manners – polite words and actions
match – two things that go together exactly
middle – the part that happens between the beginning and the end

N

nursery rhyme – a short rhyme that tells a story

O

order – how things are placed

P

picture – a painting, drawing, or photograph
prediction – what you think might happen
pretend – to make believe (e.g., when we try to fly like birds)
problem – something difficult that is happening

R

real – something that could happen or does happen
repeat – to say or do something again
rhymes – words that end with the same sound
rhythm – the beat in songs and poetry

S

same – exactly alike
senses – what living things use to learn about the world. There are five: sight, hearing, smell, taste, and touch.
sentence – group of words combined to share a thought or idea
setting – where a story takes place
shape – outline of an object (e.g., circle, square, triangle)
solution – a way of fixing a problem or difficulty
sort – to group items by something they have in common
spine – the middle part of a book's cover that holds the pages
syllable – a part of a word

T

topic – something to talk, write, or draw about

W

word family – a group of words that have the same ending sounds and spellings

Glossary for Educators & Parents

A

alliteration – the repetition of the same sounds or same kinds of sounds at the beginning of words

alliterative sentence – a sentence with repeating beginning sounds such as: "Peter Piper picked peppers."

alphabet knowledge – naming the letters of the alphabet and recognizing the written letter symbols

auditory discrimination – the ability to recognize and distinguish sounds

auditory learners – children who learn best by hearing

B

beginning sound – the first sound in a word

benchmark – A detailed description that outlines what a student is expected to know at a particular grade, age, or developmental level.

bilateral activity – a task that requires the use of both hands

blending – combining individual sounds to form words—e.g., /b/ /a/ /t/ is bat

C

categorizing – grouping items by an attribute or attributes

cognitive development – building a variety of thought processes including remembering, problem solving and decision making

compound words – a word made up of two smaller words

comprehension – making meaning from what is experienced through a variety of senses

Concepts About Print – understanding parts of a book inside and out

concrete objects – real things that children can physically touch, e.g., block, ball

cooperative learning – an instructional method that encourages children to work and learn together

D

daily life – things that happen every day

descriptive language – language that describes a person, place, thing, idea, or event

dictate – to speak while someone writes down what one is saying

direct comparison – when children compare two or more objects or ideas

directionality – knowing that English print goes top to bottom, left to right

domain – A group of related learning skills

dramatic play – pretend play where children act out different situations, usually without prompting by an adult

E

ending families – words with the same rime or ending sound

ELL (English Language Learner) – children whose first language is not English

environmental print/print awareness – understanding that print is everywhere and that reading and writing are ways to learn new ideas and information

evaluation – check for a child's understanding

expedition – an adventure to discover new things

expressive language – the ability to generate spoken words

F

final sound – the last sound in a word

formative assessments – assessments that provide feedback to guide or improve instruction

G

grouping – a collection of things that are the same

gross motor – movement using the large muscles of the body

guiding questions – questions that lead the direction of a discussion or discovery

I

independent learning – knowledge that children acquire by themselves without explicit teaching

informal assessments – casual observations or ways to collect information about children's learning

informational text – a text that has facts, ideas, and real-life stories.

initial sound – the first sound in a word

initiative – readiness to start something

K

kinesthetic learners – require movement as part of their learning process

L

language arts – listening, reading, writing, and speaking

learning skills – a detailed description that outlines what a student is expected to know at a particular grade, age, or developmental level

literacy – ability to read and write

M

manipulatives – objects used to explore ideas and solve problems, such as blocks, counters, beads, etc.

memory – ability to recall something from a previous experience

middle – the part that happens between the beginning and the end

movement perception – ability to think ahead about how one moves their own body

N

narrative skills – ability to tell a story or recount events

nursery rhyme – a short rhyme that tells a story

O

onset – a letter or group of letters that comes before the first vowel in a syllable or one-syllable word, e.g. /t/ is the onset in the words **tap** and **top**. Words or syllables beginning with vowels or silent letters do not have onsets, e.g., oar. The vowel and what comes after it is called the **rime**. (See rime.)

oral language – language that is spoken

orientation – position or direction an object or symbol faces

Glossary for Educators & Parents

P

phonological awareness – ability to hear and manipulate parts of spoken language
phonemes – the smallest sounds that make up a word
phonemic awareness – awareness of the phonemes in individual words
prior knowledge – knowledge and experiences children have before they enter school
problem-solving – ability to use various methods to determine the best answer for a problem

R

readiness – preparedness for a given skill
receptive language – ability to understand what is spoken
reversal – a letter or number symbol that is facing the wrong direction
rime – part of a syllable that consists of the vowel and the consonants that come after it, e.g., -ap, -op, and -ip are the rimes in **tap**, **top**, and **tip**. The letter(s) that comes before the vowel is called the **onset**. (See onset.)
rhyme – words that end with the same sound

S

segmentation – breaking sentences into individual words, e.g. "I hop!" can be broken into two words, "I" and "hop"; compound words into two words, e.g. "starfish" into "star" and "fish"; words into onset and rime, e.g., "mop" can be broken into the onset, /m/ and the rime, -op, and words into individual sounds or phonemes, e.g. "cat" into three individual phonemes, /k/ /a/ /t/
self-discovery – a time for children to discover things on their own about a topic
self regulation – awareness and control of one's own behavior
sequence – order in which things happen
sorting – separating objects into groups or sets based on attributes
spine – the part of the book where the front and the back meet.
syllable – a part of a word that includes a vowel sound
symbol – letter, number, or mark that represents something

T

tactile learners – children who learn best through touching materials

V

visual learners – children who learn best by seeing
visual motor control – ability to coordinate what is seen with how the body needs to respond

W

word discrimination – ability to identify individual words in a sentence

word families – same as an ending family; words that have the same endings

Index

My Book, 14, 88, 91, 95, 105, 153
music, 29, 129

names, 29, 49, 55, 63, 72–73, 74–75, 76–77, 98–99
narrative skills, 148–149
nature, 127
nursery rhymes, 38–39, 54, 55, 115, 117, 125

occupations, 109, 135, 157, 165
onset, 24, 50–51, 52–53
oral language, 36–37, 38–39, 42–43, 44–45, 48–49, 52–53, 72–73, 124–125, 126–127, 131–149, 154–155, 156–157, 158–159, 160–161, 164–165, 183
order, 108–109, 124–125
orientation, 70

parental involvement, 174–177
phonemic awareness, 25, 56–57, 58–59
phonological awareness, 23–59, 180
play, 66, 137, 154–155, 156–157, 163
plays, 113
poems, 38, 54
position, 70, 93
prediction, 105, 106–107, 115
print awareness, 92–93
print meaning, 158–159, 160–161
prior knowledge, 106–107
problem solving, 156, 162–163
problem/solution, 114–115

questioning skills, 134–135

real, 118–119, 126
re-enacting, 109, 113, 124–125, 145, 155, 157
receptive language, 21, 23, 34–35, 103, 131, 134–135, 136–137
retelling, 109, 110, 124–125, 148, 154–155, 156–157, 158–159
rime, 24, 50–51, 52–53
rhymes, 23, 29, 36–37, 38–39, 52, 55, 161
rhyming
    discriminating, 23, 37, 38
    producing, 23, 38–39
    repeating, 37
Roll–A–Dough Letters®, 63, 75

safety, 80–81, 163
same and different, 32–33, 34–35
school, 174–175
science, 153, 161
scribbling, 162–163
segmentation
    compound words, 24, 44–45, 46–47
    onset and rime, 24, 50–51, 52–53
    sentence, 24, 40–41, 42–43
    sound, 24, 30–31, 32–33
    syllables, 24, 48–49
self esteem, 171

self–regulation, 33, 171
senses, 146–147
sensory motor skills, 63, 70–71, 78–79, 80–81, 82–83, 84–85, 110–111, 116–117, 172–173
sequence, 108–109, 124–125, 159
setting, 112–113, 124
shapes, 163
signs, 67, 100–101, 162–163
Sing, Sound & Count With Me CD, 15, 26–27, 29, 31, 33, 37, 39, 41, 49, 55, 69, 99, 109, 117, 121, 125, 137, 139, 165
social behavior, 139
social-emotional development, 26–27, 66–67, 78–79, 80–81, 82–83, 84–85, 110–111, 112–113, 114–115, 116–117, 120–121, 128–129, 136–137, 138–139, 144–145, 154–155, 156–157, 162–163, 170–171, 183
Sound Around Box™, 14, 28, 34, 35, 36, 37, 39, 45, 46, 47, 50, 51, 57, 59, 67, 74, 75, 78, 79, 84, 85, 91, 141, 143, 147
sound discrimination, 30–31, 32–33
sound isolation, 56–57, 58–59
sound source, 31, 32, 33
sorting, 67, 128–129, 172
speaking etiquette, 145
spine, 92–93
sports, 121
story representation, 154–155, 156–157
story structure
    main character, 110–111, 112–113, 114–115, 120–121, 122–123, 124–125
    problem/solution, 114–115
    setting, 112–113, 124
    story tone, 116–117
syllables, 26–27, 28–29, 48–49

Tag Bags®, 77
taking turns, 72–73, 78–79, 80–81, 84–85, 110–111, 112–113, 128–129, 154–155, 156–157, 162–163, 170, 171
title, 92–93, 105
topic choice for writing, 164–165
topic of informational text, 126–127, 128–129
transitions, 171
transportation, 135
turn-taking, 72–73, 78–79, 80–81, 84–85, 110–111, 112–113, 128–129, 154–155, 156–157, 162–163, 170, 171

vocabulary instruction, 132, 133, 142–143, 160–161

Wood Pieces, 63, 75, 111, 137, 139
word discrimination, 23, 34–35
word family, 50–51, 52–53
Word Time™, 14, 97, 132, 133, 161
work, 109, 135, 157, 165
writing, 9, 151–165

References

Adams, M.J. 1990. *Beginning To Read: Thinking and Learning about Print.* Cambridge, MA: MIT Press.

Alliance for Childhood. 2006. "A Call to Action on the Education of Young Children." Retrieved from: www.allianceforchildhood.org.

Barnett, W.S., J.T. Hustedt, A.H. Friedman, J.S. Boyd, and P. Ainsworth. 2007. *The State of Preschool 2007.* New Brunswick, NJ: National Institute for Early Education Research.

Beauchat, K.A., K.L. Blamey, and S. Walpole. 2009. "Building Preschool Children's Language and Literacy One Storybook at a Time." *The Reading Teacher* 63(1):26-39.

Bergen, D. 2002. "The Role of Pretend Play in Children's Cognitive Development." *Early Childhood Research and Practice* 4(1):2-15.

Berninger, V., R.D. Abbott, J. Jones, B.J Wolf, L. Gould, M.Anderson-Youngstrom, S. Shimada, and K. Apel. 2006. "Early Development of Language by Hand: Composing, Reading, Listening, and Speaking Connections; Three Letter-Writing Modes; and Fast Mapping in Spelling." *Developmental Neuropsychology* 29:61-92.

Biemiller, A.1999. *Language and Reading Success.* Cambridge, MA: Brookline.

Bishop, D.V.M. and C. Adams.1990. "A Prospective Study of the Relationship between Specific Language Impairment, Phonological Disorders and Reading Retardation." *Journal of Child Psychology and Psychiatry and Allied Disciplines* 31:1027-1050.

Bloodgood, J.W. 1999. "What's in a Name? Children's Name Writing and Literacy Acquisition." *Reading Research Quarterly* 34(3): 342-367.

Bowman, B.T., S.M. Donovan, and S.M. Burns, editors, Commission on Behavioral and Social Sciences and Education and National Research Council. 2000. *Eager to Learn: Educating Our Preschoolers.* Washington D.C.: National Academies Press.

Chall, J. 1996. *Learning to read: The great debate.* New York: McGraw-Hill.

Chall, J.S., V.A. Jacobs, and L.E. Baldwin. 1990. *The Reading Crisis: Why Poor Children Fall Behind.* Cambridge, MA: Harvard University Press.

Christie, J.F., B.J. Enz, and C. Vukelich, 2007. *Teaching Language and Literacy: Preschool through the Elementary Grades.* Boston: Pearson Education, Inc.

Coulter, D. 1995. "Music and the Making of the Mind." *Early Childhood Connections: The Journal of Music- and Movement-Based Learning* 1:22-26.

Cunningham, A.E., and K.E. Stanovich. 1997. "Early Reading Acquisition and Its Relation to Reading Experience and Ability 10 Years Later." *Developmental Psychology* 33(6):934-945.

Dickinson, D.K., and M.W. Smith. 1994. "Long-Term Effects of Preschool Teachers' Book Readings on Low-Income Children's Vocabulary and Story Comprehension." *Reading Research Quarterly* 29:104-122.

Duncan G.J., C.J. Dowsett, A. Claessens, K. Magnuson, A.C.Huston, P. Klebanov, L.S. Pagani, L. Feinstein, M. Engel, J. Brooks-Gunn, H. Sexton, and K. Duckworth. 2007. "School Readiness and Later Achievement." *Developmental Psychology* 43(6):1428-1446.

Ellery, V. 2005. *Creating Strategic Readers: Techniques for Developing Competency in Phonemic Awareness, Phonics, Fluency, Vocabulary, and Comprehension.* Newark: International Reading Association.

Fein, G., A.E. Ardila-Rey, and L.A. Groth, 2000. "The Narrative Connection: Stories and Literacy." *Play and Literacy in Early Childhood* 27-44. Mahwah, NJ: Lawrence Erlbaum Associates.

Fox, Mem. 2001. *Reading Magic: Why Reading Aloud to Our Children Will Change Their Lives Forever.* Orlando, FL: Harcourt.

Frede, E., and D.J. Ackerman. 2007. *Preschool Curriculum Decision-Making: Dimensions to Consider."* *Preschool Policy Brief* 3(12). New Brunswick, NJ: National Institute for Early Education Research.

Gesell, A. 1940. *The First Five Years of Life: A Guide to the Study of the Preschool Child.* New York: Harper and Row.

Ginsburg, K.R. and the Committee on Communications and Committee on Psychosocial Aspects of Child and Family Health. 2006. Clinical report: "The Importance of Play in Promoting Healthy Child Development and Maintaining Strong Parent-Child Bonds." *American Academy of Pediatrics.* Retrieved from: www.aap.org/pressroom/playFINAL.pdf.

Healy, J. 2004. *Your Child's Growing Mind: Brain Development and Learning from Birth to Adolescence.* New York: Three Rivers Press.

Hirsh-Pasek, K., R. Golinkoff, L. Berk, and D. Singer. 2008. *A Manifesto for Playful Learning in Preschool: Presenting the Scientific Evidence.* New York: Oxford.

Honig, B. 2001. *Teaching our Children to Read.* Thousand Oaks, CA: Corwin Press.

International Reading Association and the National Association for the Education of Young Children. 1998. Joint Position Statement: *Learning to Read and Write: Developmentally Appropriate Practices for Young Children.* Washington, D.C.: International Reading Association.

Isenberg, J., and N. Quisenberry, 2002. Position paper: *Play: Essential for All Children.* Association for Childhood Education International. Retrieved from: www.acei.org/playpaper.htm.

Jensen, E. 2001. *Arts with the Brain in Mind.* Alexandria, VA: Association for Supervision and Curriculum Development.

Johnston, F. R. 2004. "Phonics, Phonological Awareness, and the Alphabet." *EPS Update,* April. http://eps.schoolspecialty.com/downloads/articles/phonological_awareness.pdf.

Jones, E. and R. Cooper. 2006. *Playing to Get Smart.* New York: Teachers College Press.

Juel, C. 1988. "Learning to Read and Write: A Longitudinal Study of Fifty-Four Children from First through Fourth Grade." *Journal of Educational Psychology* 80:437-447.

Juel, C., P.L Griffith, and P.B. Gough. 1986. "Acquisition of Literacy: A Longitudinal Study of Children in First and Second Grade." *Journal of Educational Psychology* 78:243-255.

Kim, S. 1999. "The Effects of Storytelling and Pretend Play on Cognitive Processes, Short-Term and Long-Term Narrative Recall." *Child Study Journal* 29(3):175-191.

Lonigan, C.J. 2008. "(Almost) Everything You Wanted to Know about Phonological Awareness and Were Afraid to Ask." Paper presented at the Early Reading First Grantee Meeting, New Orleans, LA.

Lonigan, C.J., S.R. Burgess, and J.L. Anthony. 2000. "Development of Emergent Literacy and Early Reading Skills in Preschool Children: Evidence from a Latent-Variable Longitudinal Study." *Developmental Psychology* 36:596-613.

Lonigan, C.J., and T. Shanahan. 2009. *Developing Early Literacy: Report of the National Early Literacy Panel.* Jessup, MD: National Institute for Literacy. Retrieved from: http://lincs.ed.gov/publications/pdf/NELPReport09.pdf.

Maclean, M., P. Bryant, and L. Bradley, 1987. "Rhymes, Nursery Rhymes, and Reading in Early Childhood." *Merrill-Palmer Quarterly* 33:255-282.

McAfee, O., D.J. Leong, and E. Bodrova. 2004. *Basics of Assessment: A Primer for Early Childhood Educators.* Washington, D.C.: National Association for the Education of Young Children.

Morrison, F., and R. Cooney, 2002. "Parenting and Academic Achievement: Multiple Paths to Early Literacy." *Parenting and the Children's World: Influences on Academic, Intellectual, and Social-Emotional Development* 141-160. Mahwah, NJ: Lawrence Erlbaum.

Morrow, L. 2005. *"Literacy Development in the Early Years: Helping Children Read and Write."* Boston: Allyn & Bacon.

National Association for the Education of Young Children. 2009. Position statement: *Developmentally Appropriate Practice in Early Childhood Programs Serving Children from Birth through Age 8.* Washington, DC: National Association for the Education of Young Children.

National Association for the Education of Young Children and the National Association of Early Childhood Specialists in State Departments of Education. 2003. Joint position statement: *Early Childhood Curriculum, Assessment, and Program Evaluation: Building an Effective, Accountable System in Programs for Children Birth through Age 8.* Retrieved from: www.naeyc.org/about/positions/pdf/CAPEexpand.pdf.

National Association for the Education of Young Children & the International Reading Association. 1998. "Learning to Read and Write: Developmentally Appropriate Practices for Young Children." *Young Children* 53(4):30-46. Retrieved from www.naeyc.org/files/naeyc/file/positions/PSREAD98.pdf.

National Association of State Boards of Education. 2006. *Fulfilling the Promise of Preschool: The Report of the NASBE Study Group on Creating High-Quality Early Learning Environments.* National Child Care Information and Technical Assistance Center.

National Institute of Child Health & Human Development. 2000. *Report of the National Reading Panel: Teaching Children to Read: An Evidence-Based Assessment of the Scientific Research Literature on Reading and Its Implications for Reading Instruction.* Washington, D.C.: U.S. Government Printing Office.

National Institute for Early Education Research. 2005. *Promoting Children's Social and Emotional Development through Preschool Education.* Washington, D.C. Retrieved from nieer.org/resources/policyreports/report7.pdf.

Olsen, J. Z., and E. F. Knapton. 2008. *Pre-K Teacher's Guide.* Cabin John, MD: Handwriting Without Tears.

Pica, R. 2008. "Learning by Leaps and Bounds: Why Motor Skills Matter." *Young Children* 63(4):48-9.

Rubin, K.H., W. Bukowski, and K. Parker. 2006. "Peer Interactions, Relationships, and Groups." *Handbook of Child Psychology: Social, Emotional, and Personality Development* 571-645. New York: Wiley.

Scarborough, H. S. 2001. "Connecting Early Language and Literacy to Later Reading (Dis)abilities: Evidence, Theory, and Practice." *Handbook of Early Literacy Research* 97-110. New York: The Guilford Press.

Scarborough, H.S. 1991. "Early Syntactic Development of Dyslexic Children." *Annals of Dyslexia* 41:207-220.

Scarborough, H.S. 1990. "Very Early Language Deficits in Dyslexic Children." *Child Development* 61:1728-1743.

Schickedanz, J.A., and R.M. Casbergue. 2004. *Writing in Preschool: Learning to Orchestrate Meaning and Marks.* Newark, DE: International Reading Association.

The Albert Shanker Institute. 2009. *Preschool Curriculum: What's in It for Children and Teachers.* Washington, D.C. Retrieved from www.ashankerinst.org/Downloads/Early Childhood 12-11-08.pdf.

Shonkoff, J. and D. Phillips, D., eds. 2000. *From Neurons to Neighborhoods: The Science of Early Childhood Development.* Washington: National Academies Press.

Silverman, R., and J. DiBara Crandell, 2010. "Vocabulary Practices in Prekindergarten and Kindergarten Classrooms." *Reading Research Quarterly* 45(3):318-340.

Singer, D.G., R. Golinkoff, and K. Hirsh-Pasek, eds. 2006. *Play = Learning: How Play Motivates and Enhances Children's Cognitive and Social-Emotional Growth.* New York: Oxford University Press.

Singer, D. G., J. L. Singer, S.L. Plaskon, and A.E. Schweder. 2003. "The Role of Play in the Preschool Curriculum." *All Work and No Play: How Educational Reforms are Harming Our Preschoolers* 43-70. Westport, CT: Praeger.

Snow, C.E., W.S. Barnes, J. Chandler, I.F. Goodman, and L. Hemphill. 1991. *Unfulfilled Expectations: Home and School Influences on Literacy.* Cambridge, MA: Harvard University Press.

Snow, C.E., M.S. Burns, and P. Griffin, eds. 1998. *Preventing Reading Difficulties in Young Children.* Washington, D.C.: National Academies Press.

Snow, C.E., P. Tabors, P. Nicholson, and B. Kirkland. 1995. "SHELL: Oral Language and Early Literacy Skills in Kindergarten and First-Grade Children." *Journal of Research in Childhood Education* 10:37-48.

Spear-Swerling, L. 2006. "Children's Reading Comprehension and Oral Reading Fluency in Easy Text." *Reading & Writing: An Interdisciplinary Journal* 19:199-220.

Stahl, S.A., and B.A. Murray. 1994. "Defining Phonological Awareness and Its Relationship to Early Reading." *Journal of Educational Psychology* 86(2):221-234.

Stanovich, K.E. 1986. "Matthew Effects in Reading: Some Consequences of Individual Differences in the Acquisition of Literacy." *Reading Research Quarterly* 21:360-407.

Stanovich, K.E. 1993. "Romance and Reality." *Reading Teacher* 47(4):280-91.

Stevenson, H.W., and R.S. Newman. 1986. "Long-Term Prediction of Achievement and Attitude in Mathematics and Reading." *Child Development* 57:646-659.

Storch, S. A., G.J. Whitehurst. 2002. "Oral Language and Code-Related Precursors to Reading: Evidence from a Longitudinal Structural Model." *Developmental Psychology* 38:934-947.

Treiman, R. 1993. *Beginning to Spell: A Study of First-Grade Children.* New York: Oxford University Press.

Vukelich, C., and J. Christie. 2004. *Building a Foundation for Preschool Literacy: Effective Instruction for Children's Reading and Writing Development.* Newark: International Reading Association.

Walker D., C. Greenwood, B. Hart, and J. Carta. 1994. "Prediction of School Outcomes Based on Early Language Production and Socioeconomic Factors." *Child Development* 65:606-621.

Wasik, B.A. 2010. "What Teachers Can Do to Promote Preschoolers' Vocabulary Development: Strategies From an Effective Language and Literacy Professional Development Coaching Model." *The Reading Teacher* 63(8):621-633.

West, J., K. Denton, E. Germino-Hausken. 2000. *America's Kindergarteners.* Washington, D.C.: U.S. Department of Education, Office of Educational Research and Improvement, National Center for Education Statistics. Retrieved from http://nces.ed.gov/pubs2000/2000070.pdf.

West, J., K. Denton, and L. Reaney. 2001. *The Kindergarten Year.* Washington, D.C.: National Center for Education Statistics.

Whitehurst, G. J., and C.J. Lonigan, 1998. "Child Development and Emergent Literacy." *Child Development* 69:848-872.